I0605707

'A truly beautiful book, written by my favourite Spanish man. These pages are packed with joyful rays of inspiration and utter deliciousness.'

Jamie Oliver

Recipes from Catalonia

This book is dedicated to Peter, for his amazing help in many different ways but especially his input in researching the food and locations, which was crucial.

Also, to my mum and dad, my sister, Isabel, my brother, Antonio, my sister-in-law, Maria José, and my nieces and nephews, Carmen, Juan, Mariana, Cristina and Antonio – you have always been there for me and I love you all.

Introduction

Catalonia is really beautiful. I have visited so many times over the years and one thing I know for sure is the more I go, the more I love this place and the people. Doing research for this book has allowed me to become more and more familiar with the particular diversity and richness of the animals on the land, the stunning produce in the sea, and the wonderful birds in the air. I want to share with you here in my book some of the region's gastronomic treasures because they are culinary gems, and food, after all, is all about sharing.

I have travelled from Roses in Girona to Balaguer in Lleida, from Vilafranca del Penedès in Barcelona to Sant Carles de la Ràpita in Tarragona. My trips have been about visiting old friends, as well as meeting new people and making new friends, all of whom gladly opened their homes and their hearts to us. I've been discovering and learning about the cities, towns and villages while uncovering some amazing culinary secrets (not all disclosed, of course!). Catalonia has a fascinating history that includes political and social struggles to hold on to a unique identity, and a rich culture and heritage. I was inspired to learn that often the most challenging times seemed to strengthen their resolve and make their cultural heritage even more important and more dearly cherished. Catalonia is a place where visitors often describe feeling 'at home'. It's a very welcoming place.

In this book, I really hope to have captured something of the essential flavours found in the gastronomy of Catalonia; and, when you try some of the recipes, my wish is that you will also share in the enjoyment of dishes that, for me, reflect the heart of both traditional and contemporary Catalan cuisine.

Something I love is that, in their cooking, the people of Catalonia have never lost their culinary roots – sometimes aspects of recipes or methods stretch as far back as medieval times. There are many stunning dishes that bring together dried fruit and meat, a mix of meat and seafood, and the clever use of spices in different ways. In Catalan cuisine, there's often a healthy nod to history, and this I really love – in the food, we see that the people are so proud of their heritage and cultural identity and love who they are and where they're from. When you try some of the dishes in my book, I hope you too will get a sense of the creativity that has been passed down from generation to generation. In this way, food really fascinates me – it's like a wonderful way of encoding and capturing history and culture on a plate, and offering these handed-down recipes to others, trusting the cooks and the consumers to experience something of the labour of culinary love they also received.

In this book, I bring together a variety of old and new recipes based on my discovery of some fabulous ingredients from some of the most beautiful, crystal-clear waters and lush green mountains. I want you to feel how I feel in Catalonia, inspired by the great people and stunning places. My food adventures have been such a privilege and a pleasure, and I've loved every minute of it. I sincerely hope you will enjoy this book too.

Meat

To enjoy cooking and then eating the meat of animals that have been well bred, well fed and, above all, well cared for, is simply a privilege. Catalonia has such a diverse range of farmland and climates, from the greener mountains of Pirineo de Lleida to the wet marshlands of Delta del Ebro, that it's easy to find meat with incredible provenance and an amazing flavour. There's a whole range of meat dishes in this chapter, some that I hope might become staple recipes that you go back to and others that are a bit more for special occasions. Either way, always try to source the best-quality meat you can – it's worth it.

If you are in the L'Empordà area of Catalonia, then you must stay at Mas Rabiol, a gorgeous *masia* (old farm) run by Gloria and Carlos. The place and the food are beautiful, with great Catalan cooking, not least the delicious breakfast. A huge selection of local cheeses and *butifarras*, golden olive oil and proper bread greets you in the morning – the perfect start to the day. Butifarra is a Catalan speciality – a fresh sausage traditionally made from raw pork meat, salt and pepper.

One of the best things I've had there is Gloria's *escudella*. Escudella is a one-pot meal, traditionally made with dried chickpeas (garbanzos) and lots of different cuts of meat. In this recipe I haven't used chickpeas, but if you would like to, you can add 400 g (14 oz) at the same time as the meat – just soak them in cold water for 12 hours first.

If you're going to Mas Rabiol, be sure to ask Gloria to make this for you before you get there, as it takes a little while to prepare. When I go with my partner it's always the first thing we ask for.

Escudella, my way

Serves 6

2 onions, peeled and sliced
2 carrots, quartered
2 celery stalks, chopped
2 bay leaves
handful of parsley stalks
10 black peppercorns
1 ham hock
4 chicken legs
2 butifarra sausages (or other large sausages), sliced
2 beef short ribs
300 g (10½ oz) small pasta
sea salt and freshly ground black pepper

Put all the ingredients except for the pasta in a large pan and cover with water. Bring to the boil, then reduce the heat to a gentle simmer and cook, uncovered, for 2 hours until the meat is extremely tender.

Remove the meat with a slotted spoon and shred, discarding any skin and bones. Bring the liquid to a boil, season well, add the pasta and cook for 10–12 minutes until al dente.

Return the meat to the pan and serve.

Almost everyone loves jamón croquetas, and they're one of the biggest sellers in my restaurants. But we also like to play around with new flavours too – sometimes a bit crazy, but they normally work and everyone loves them!

If you're a fan of mint, add some at the same time as the apple and morcilla, and you'll have a really fresh flavour.

Black pudding & apple croquetas

Makes 16–20

500 ml (17 fl oz) whole (full-fat) milk
150 ml (5 fl oz) fresh vegetable stock
85 g (3 oz) butter, plus an extra knob
120 g (4 oz/scant 1 cup) plain (all-purpose) flour
75 g (2½ oz) manchego cheese, grated
150 g (5½ oz) morcilla, chopped
1 apple, peeled, cored and finely chopped
sprinkle of caster (superfine) sugar
150 g (5½ oz/1½ cups) dry breadcrumbs
2 large (extra large) free-range eggs, beaten
olive oil for deep-frying
sea salt and freshly ground black pepper

Heat the milk and stock together in a saucepan. In another saucepan melt the butter over a medium heat, add the flour and cook for 2–3 minutes until browned. Gradually add the milk and stock mixture, until you have a thick, smooth béchamel sauce. Season to taste and add the cheese. Stir until melted and smooth. Set aside.

Meanwhile, heat a little oil in a pan and fry the morcilla until starting to crisp, then drain on kitchen paper. Add a knob of butter to the pan and, when foaming, add the apple and sugar and cook for a couple of minutes until lightly caramelised. Fold the morcilla and apple into the béchamel.

Spread the mixture out evenly in a shallow tray and press down. Cover with a sheet of baking parchment or cling film (plastic wrap). Chill in the fridge for at least 2 hours.

Put some oil in the palm of your hand and roll the mixture into balls of 30 g (1 oz) each. Put the breadcrumbs and eggs in two separate bowls. Dip the croquetas first in the eggs and then in the breadcrumbs to coat all over.

Heat the oil in a deep pan to 190°C (375°F) – or until a cube of bread browns in about 20 seconds – and fry the croquetas for around 2 minutes or until golden. Place on kitchen paper to drain. Devour immediately.

TERRY

In the beautiful Delta del Ebro, where you can find some of the best rice in the Iberian Peninsula, there is a wonderful restaurant called L'Estany, which I love. I was taken there by Lola and José Miguel; they are locals and know the area well. José Miguel is a rice farmer, which has been his family's business for a long time.

I've tested this recipe using wild rabbit. However, farmed rabbit is easier to find but larger in size. If you use this instead, just cook the meat in the stock for around 1 hour, or until the meat is falling apart.

Rabbit rice

Serves 4–6

1 wild rabbit, jointed into 6 (ask your butcher to do this for you)
olive oil for frying
1 large onion, finely chopped
2 celery stalks, finely chopped
2 garlic cloves, sliced
1 red chilli, deseeded and finely chopped
pinch of saffron threads
1.4 litres (2½ pints) fresh chicken stock
250 g (9 oz/1⅛ cups) Japonica rice or paella rice
sea salt and freshly ground black pepper

Season the rabbit to taste and fry in a large frying pan in a little olive oil to brown all over. Remove from the pan and set aside. Add a little more oil and fry the onion and celery for 10 minutes. Then add the garlic and chilli and fry for 10 minutes more. Add the saffron and stir to mix. Then add 1.2 litres (2 pints) of the stock and bring to a simmer. Return the rabbit to the pan, cover and simmer for 45 minutes until really tender and falling apart.

Stir in the rice and the rest of the stock, season, cover and simmer gently for 15–18 minutes without stirring, until it is just cooked but still a little soupy. Serve spooned into bowls.

Butifarra is a traditional Catalan sausage, made from raw pork meat, salt and pepper. There are now many different versions, including black butifarra and even a sweet one too.

We have one at my restaurant which has ceps in it – we simply cook it on the plancha, and then serve it with chickpeas (garbanzos) and green beans. *Botifarra amb mongetes* is Catalan for butifarra and beans. In Catalonia they don't serve the beans with vegetables or stock. This recipe, however, is how I make it in the restaurants for staff, and we really love it! The vegetables taste great.

Fresh butifarra with beans

Serves 4

olive oil for frying
1 large onion, finely chopped
1 carrot, finely chopped
1 celery stalk, finely chopped
2 garlic cloves, finely sliced
200 ml (7 fl oz) fresh vegetable stock
sea salt and freshly ground black pepper
4 large black or white butifarra sausages (or other large sausages)
handful of chopped parsley
sea salt and freshly ground black pepper

for the beans

250 g (9 oz) dried white beans, soaked overnight in cold water
1 carrot, quartered
1 leek, halved
1 celery stalk, roughly chopped
1 bay leaf
10 black peppercorns

Drain the beans and put in a large pan with the carrot, leek, celery, bay leaf and peppercorns. Cover with 2½ litres (5¼ pints) of cold water. Bring to the boil, then simmer for 1–1½ hours until the beans are just tender. Drain and discard the vegetables, bay leaf and peppercorns.

When the beans are ready, heat a little oil in a pan and fry the onion, carrot and celery for 15 minutes until really softened. Add the garlic and fry for a minute more, then add the drained beans and vegetable stock. Season well and simmer for 10 minutes.

Meanwhile, fry the sausages in a pan with a little oil until they are browned all over and cooked through. Stir the parsley into the beans and serve with the sausages.

A great example of a *mar y montaña* – sea and mountain – recipe, this dish always goes down a treat when I put it on the menu at my restaurants.

If you can't get really good-quality Ibérico pork mincemeat, just use the best minced (ground) pork that you can find.

As you may know, you must cook squid and cuttlefish either very slowly or very quickly. Here we're cooking it really slowly so it's lovely and tender.

Meatballs with cuttlefish

Serves 6

200 g (7 oz) minced (ground) pork
200 g (7 oz) minced (ground) beef
3 garlic cloves, 1 crushed and 2 finely sliced
handful of parsley, finely chopped
handful of thyme sprigs, leaves stripped
75 g (2½ oz/scant 1 cup) fresh white breadcrumbs
1 free-range egg
olive oil for frying
plain (all-purpose) flour, to dust
1 large fresh cuttlefish (about 1 kg/2 lb 4 oz), cleaned and cut into thin strips
2 onions, finely chopped
450 g (1 lb) chopped fresh tomatoes
250 ml (8 fl oz) fresh chicken stock
sea salt and freshly ground black pepper

In a large bowl, mix the two lots of minced meat with the crushed garlic, parsley, thyme, breadcrumbs and egg. Season well and mix together, then shape into small meatballs. Refrigerate for 30 minutes.

Heat a little oil in a pan, dust the meatballs with flour and fry until golden brown and nearly cooked through. Remove from the pan and set aside.

Heat a little more oil over a high heat and fry the cuttlefish until browned all over. Remove with a slotted spoon and set aside.

Add the onions to the pan and fry for 10 minutes before adding the sliced garlic and tomatoes. Cook for 10 minutes more, then add the stock and return the cuttlefish to the pan. Season well and simmer very gently for 1 hour or until very, very tender.

Add the meatballs and simmer for 5–10 minutes until they are nice and hot. Serve straightaway.

The inspiration for this recipe came from Carlos at Mas Rabiol in L'Empordà, Girona, where they make a gorgeous trotter burger without any bread, and use just the meat. However, this idea sprang to mind, and it is one of the best sliders I have ever eaten.

Trotter sliders

Makes 14–16 sliders (6–8 burgers)

3 pig's trotters
1 onion, roughly chopped
1 carrot, roughly chopped
1 celery stalk, chopped
1 bay leaf
handful of parsley stalks
handful of black peppercorns
400 g (14 oz) minced (ground) pork
2 garlic cloves
2 tablespoons finely chopped oregano
small handful of chopped parsley
sea salt and freshly ground black pepper
olive oil for frying

to serve
mini brioche buns or slider buns
1 quantity alioli (page 154)
1 quantity romesco sauce (page 146)

Put the trotters with the vegetables, bay leaf, parsley and peppercorns in a large pan of cold water. Bring to the boil and then simmer very gently for 4 hours until really tender. Drain and discard the liquid, vegetables, herbs and peppercorns.

When cool enough to handle, remove the skin from the trotters. Pick all the meat and fat from the bones and put in a bowl with the minced pork. Discard the bones and gristle. Finely chop the skin and add to the bowl of meat.

Add the garlic, oregano and parsley to the meat mix and combine well with lots of seasoning. Shape into 6–8 burgers or 14–16 small sliders. Chill in the fridge for 30 minutes.

Heat a layer of oil in a pan and fry the burgers until golden brown all over and piping hot. Toast the buns and spread with alioli and romesco sauce. Serve the burgers in the buns and eat immediately.

Civet is what the Catalans call stew, a classic dish that I have cooked many times. It's perfect for those cold winter evenings, or whenever you just fancy something comforting.

This civet, stew, or whatever you would like to call it, is great with a glass of Costers del Segre, from the wine region of Lleida.

Civet of venison with ceps

Serves 6

1.5 kg (3 lb 5 oz) haunch of venison, cut into large pieces
660 ml (23 fl oz) Spanish lager
1 carrot, finely chopped
1 celery stalk, finely chopped
1 onion, finely chopped
2 garlic cloves, peeled
1 bay leaf
2–3 sprigs of thyme
olive oil for frying
200 g (7 oz) chorizo, cut into chunks
500 ml (17 fl oz) fresh beef stock
25 g (1 oz) dried ceps
sea salt and freshly ground black pepper

Put the venison in a bowl with the lager and all the vegetables and herbs. Leave to marinate for 3–6 hours. Drain, saving the liquid and vegetables separately.

Pat the meat dry with kitchen paper and season well. Heat a layer of oil in a casserole dish (Dutch oven) and brown the venison and chorizo all over. Remove with a slotted spoon and set aside. Add a little more oil and fry the reserved vegetables for 10 minutes, then return the meat to the dish with the reserved marinade. Bubble for a few minutes, then add the stock and bring to a simmer. Cover and cook for 2–2½ hours until the meat is very tender.

Soak the ceps in 150 ml (5 fl oz) of boiling water until softened. Drain, reserving the liquid, and roughly chop. When the stew is nearly done, add the ceps and reserved soaking liquid and finish cooking. Serve with creamy mash.

A classic *mar y moñtana* – sea and mountain – dish. Some people say there is a legend that a farmer fell in love with a mermaid, and from that love came the mix of sea and land. I don't know if it is true or not, but this recipe is just delicious!

Chicken stew with langoustines

Serves 4–6

olive oil for frying
10–12 fresh langoustines
8 chicken thighs, skin left on
good knob of butter
4 large onions, finely chopped
2 fresh tomatoes, diced
3 garlic cloves, finely sliced
1 bay leaf
200 ml (7 fl oz) white wine
2 tablespoons sherry vinegar
400 ml (14 fl oz) fresh chicken stock
few sprigs of fresh tarragon
sea salt and freshly ground black pepper

Heat a little oil in a large pan with a lid. Add the langoustines and cook for 2–3 minutes. Remove and set aside. Season the chicken to taste and add to the pan. Brown all over, then remove and set aside.

Add a little more oil and a good knob of butter to the pan. Fry the onions very, very gently for 20–30 minutes until really soft and caramelised. Add the tomatoes, garlic and bay leaf and cook for 10 minutes more. Add the wine and vinegar and bubble for a minute, then add the stock and tarragon.

Return the chicken and any juices to the pan, cover and simmer for 15 minutes until the chicken is almost cooked. Add the langoustines to the pan and cook for a couple of minutes more. Serve with crusty bread to mop up the juices.

17

Chocolate is well used in Catalan cooking, often to thicken sauces. This type of sauce is called a *picada*. Normally you use dried fruit, garlic and parsley. You might think it's crazy, but I have a great recipe where I add chocolate to prawns (shrimp) that are sautéed with chilli and garlic. Yum!

Pollo with chocolate

Serves 4

olive oil for frying
1 large (extra large) free-range chicken (1.8 kg/3 lb 15 oz)
2 onions, finely sliced
2 garlic cloves
100 ml (3½ fl oz) white wine
100 ml (3½ fl oz) vino rancio (or a manzanilla sherry)
2–3 fresh tomatoes, chopped
1 bouquet garni or a bunch of herbs, tied (e.g. fresh thyme sprigs, bay leaf, parsley stalks and oregano)
1 cinnamon stick
900 ml (31½ fl oz) fresh chicken stock
sea salt and freshly ground black pepper

for the picada
olive oil for frying
80 g (2¾ oz) stale white bread, cut into small pieces
1 garlic clove
1 chicken liver
pinch of saffron threads
small handful of chopped parsley
20 g (¾ oz) grated dark chocolate (minimum 70% cocoa solids)
30 g (1 oz) hazelnuts

Preheat the oven to 150°C (300°F/Gas 2).

Heat a layer of oil in a large casserole dish (Dutch oven) and brown the chicken all over. Remove and set aside. Add the onions to the dish and fry for 10 minutes until softened. Add the garlic and cook for a minute more, then splash in the white wine and vino rancio and cook for a further 2–3 minutes.

Add the tomatoes, bouquet garni, cinnamon and stock. Season well and bring to the boil. Return the chicken to the dish and cover. Cook in the oven for 1–1½ hours until really tender.

Meanwhile, make the picada. Heat a little oil in a pan and fry the bread, garlic and chicken liver for 2–3 minutes. Tip into a food processor or use a pestle and mortar. Soak the saffron for a few minutes in 50 ml (2 fl oz) of boiling water, then add this to the bread mixture with the parsley, chocolate and hazelnuts. Whiz or pound to a paste.

When the chicken is cooked (the juices will run clear when you pierce the thickest part with a skewer), remove from the oven and lift the bird onto a plate to rest. Put the casserole dish over a medium heat and add the picada to the sauce. Whisk together and bubble until the sauce is thickened. Carve the chicken and serve with the sauce.

I've never published a book with a goose recipe in it, mainly because goose doesn't seem to be that popular. I think it's delicious, though, and worth the investment once in a while.

Using dried fruit is a really Mediterranean thing to do, and it's usually done with chicken, so here's a bit of a change. *Disfruta* – enjoy.

Roast goose with dried fruit sauce

Serves 4–6

1 goose (about 4 kg/8 lb 13 oz)
1 apple, quartered
1 orange, halved
small bunch of mixed herbs (parsley, thyme, rosemary)
sea salt and freshly ground black pepper

for the sauce
250 g (9 oz) chopped mixed dried fruit (apricots, sultanas, prunes, apples)
juice of 1 orange
150 ml (5 fl oz) sweet wine
olive oil for frying
2 shallots, finely chopped
1 garlic clove, finely sliced
500 ml (17 fl oz) fresh chicken stock
handful of chopped parsley

Preheat the oven to 180°C (350°F/Gas 4).

Put the goose in a large roasting tin on a trivet. Put the apple inside the goose, squeeze orange juice over the bird and put the orange halves and the herbs inside with the apple. Season the whole bird generously. Pour 150 ml (5 fl oz) of water into the tin under the goose and roast for 2–2½ hours until golden and cooked (the juices will run clear when you pierce the thickest part with a skewer).

Meanwhile, prepare the sauce. Put the dried fruit in a pan with the orange juice and wine. Bring to a simmer, then remove from the heat and set aside for the fruit to absorb the flavours and liquid.

Heat a little olive oil in another pan and fry the shallots for 10 minutes, then add the garlic and the soaked fruit. Add the stock and simmer for 15 minutes. Season and stir in the parsley.

When the goose is cooked, transfer to a dish to rest. Skim the fat from the juices in the tin, then add the juices to the sauce. Slice the goose and serve with the dried fruit sauce.

This is the perfect, warming salad to have on a cold autumn or winter evening, but it's also great served cold, so have it *tienes ganas* – whenever you like!

If you can get wild duck, it brings a whole other dimension to the dish. We have used farmed duck here because it is easy to find but just cook for a little less time if you're using wild duck as they are normally a bit smaller.

Warm duck, pumpkin & pardina lentil salad

Serves 4

olive oil for frying
knob of butter
700 g (1 lb 9 oz) pumpkin (squash), cut into small pieces
300 g (10½ oz) Spanish pardina lentils
½ cinnamon stick
1 garlic clove
500 ml (17 fl oz) fresh chicken stock
2 duck breasts, skin scored
wild rocket (arugula) or spicy leaves
handful of finely chopped parsley
sea salt and freshly ground black pepper

for the dressing
1 tablespoon sherry vinegar
1 tablespoon red wine vinegar
1 teaspoon Dijon mustard
3–4 tablespoons extra virgin olive oil

Preheat the oven to 200°C (400°F/Gas 6).

Heat the oil and butter in a pan and fry the pumpkin for 15–20 minutes until caramelised and tender. Set aside.

Put the lentils in a pan with the cinnamon, garlic and stock, bring to the boil and simmer for 20 minutes until tender. Drain and discard the cinnamon and garlic.

Season the duck with plenty of salt and pepper and put, skin side down, in an ovenproof pan over a low heat. Cook slowly until the fat has rendered out and it is golden and crispy. Turn the breasts over and put the pan in the oven for 6–8 minutes until the duck is cooked but pink in the centre. Set aside to rest.

To make the dressing, whisk the vinegars with plenty of seasoning and the mustard. Gradually whisk in the oil to form a glossy dressing.

Toss the lentils and pumpkin together. Slice the duck and add any juices to the dressing. Pour the dressing over the lentils and mix with the rocket and parsley. Serve with the sliced duck.

La bomba de la Barceloneta is one of the most popular tapas in Barcelona. It's a big fried ball made with mashed potato and normally stuffed with spicy carrots or meat.

I'm not sure if it's true, but La Cova Fumada is renowned as the birthplace of this dish. It is definitely worth a visit – it's a lovely old-fashioned bar serving great food. Enjoy a *vermut* with your *bomba* – they cook a stunning local version with prawns (shrimp) and octopus, which is very tasty.

La Barceloneta was badly destroyed during the Spanish Civil War, as was the area in London where I have two of my restaurants, Bermondsey, in World War II. We've used a little bit of irony here, and called this dish the 'Bermondsey Bomb' as it appears on my menu.

Bermondsey bomb

Makes 6

1 kg (2 lb 4 oz) Desiree potatoes
4 tablespoons olive oil
2 onions, finely chopped
1 large garlic clove, finely chopped
2 good pinches of chilli flakes
400 g (14 oz) tin tomatoes
160 g (5½ oz) minced (ground) pork
75 g (2½ oz/scant ⅔ cup) plain (all-purpose) flour
2 free-range eggs, beaten
100 g (3½ oz/1 cup) dry breadcrumbs
olive oil for deep-frying
1 quantity alioli (page 154), to serve
sea salt and freshly ground black pepper

Put the potatoes in a large pan with cold salted water and bring to the boil. When cooked through, drain and let cool. Peel and mash the potatoes. Season to taste and set aside. Keep warm.

Meanwhile, heat 2 tablespoons of the olive oil in a saucepan and add half of the onions. Cook over a medium heat until they start to caramelise (about 20–30 minutes), then add the garlic and a pinch of chilli flakes. Cook for another minute and then add the meat. Cook for 10 minutes and season to taste. Set aside.

To make the spicy tomato sauce, heat the remaining olive oil in another pan and cook the rest of the onions over a medium heat until soft. Add a pinch of chilli flakes and the tomatoes and cook until reduced, with almost no juices left. Season to taste.

Make a ball of around 100 g (3½ oz) mash. Use your thumb to press a hole into the centre. Fill the cavity with the meat mixture and cover with more mash to enclose the filling. Repeat with the remaining mash and meat mixture.

Put the flour, eggs and breadcrumbs in separate bowls. One by one, roll the balls first in the flour, then in the egg and finally in the breadcrumbs.

In a deep pan heat enough oil to cover two to three 'bombs' to 180°C (350°F) or until a cube of bread browns in 20 seconds. Fry the bombs until golden – use a thermometer to make sure they are hot inside. Spoon some alioli in the centre of a plate and place a bomb on top, then spoon over the spicy tomato sauce. Serve hot.

This is a really traditional beef stew, which some say originated in France. I was given this recipe by Monty, my right-hand man in the kitchen, and a great young chef with a lot of love for his Catalonia country.

Fricandó of beef with pied bleu mushrooms & black olives

Serves 6

60 ml (2 fl oz) olive oil
1.2 kg (2 lb 10 oz) beef shin in large pieces
1 large onion, finely chopped
1 carrot, finely chopped
1 celery stalk, finely chopped
500 g (1 lb 2 oz) fresh tomatoes, chopped
100 ml (3½ fl oz) brandy
500 ml (17 fl oz) fresh beef stock
200 g (7 oz) pied bleu mushrooms
150 g (5½ oz) black olives, pitted
sea salt and freshly ground black pepper

for the picada
olive oil for frying
1 slice bread
25 g (1 oz) hazelnuts
25 g (1 oz) almonds
1 garlic clove

Heat most of the oil in a casserole dish (Dutch oven). Season the beef to taste and brown in the dish. Remove with a slotted spoon and set aside.

Add the remaining oil to the dish and fry the onion, carrot and celery for 10 minutes until softened. Add the tomatoes and cook for 10 minutes more.

Return the meat to the dish and splash in the brandy. Bubble for a minute, then add the stock. Season to taste, then cover and simmer gently for 2½–3 hours.

Meanwhile, make the picada. Heat a little oil in a pan and fry the bread until golden. Whiz in a blender with the rest of the picada ingredients and enough oil to make a paste. Set aside.

When the beef is nearly done, heat a little oil in a pan and fry the mushrooms until golden. Add to the casserole with the picada and continue cooking for 20 minutes until the beef is tender and the sauce thick. Add the olives and serve.

When I was a child, I was so envious of my friend Elsa as she always knew the best place to find snails. It took a lot of spying on her, but eventually I found the spot. Snails weren't popular to eat in Talaván, so I just used to bring them back and put them in my mum's garden. One day Mum realised what I'd been doing and she was so mad – all the snails had been eating her plants!

I love to eat them now, and the best I've ever had are from Priorat, where they cook them over a fire with plenty of garlic oil.

Snails with garlic & parsley oil

Serves 4 as a starter

24 g (1 oz) fresh and purged snails
small glass white wine
6 garlic cloves, crushed
large bunch of finely chopped parsley
100 ml (3½ fl oz) extra virgin olive oil
sea salt and freshly ground black pepper

Heat a large pan over a high heat. Add the snails and wine and cover and cook for 2–3 minutes until just cooked. Drain.

Mix the garlic with the parsley and oil and plenty of seasoning. Remove the snails from their shells. Divide half the oil between the shells, then put the snails back in and spread the rest of the oil over the top.

Heat a snail tray or cast-iron pan over a high heat and cook the snails for another 2–3 minutes until they are piping hot. Serve straightaway with lots of bread.

Over time, the local Catalonian breeds of pig have sadly disappeared. I've recently had some amazing meat from a new breed, El Ral d'Avinyó, which has been bred by some really innovative butchers in the region, but some great-quality British pork will work perfectly for this recipe.

Pork belly usually feels quite wintry, but I think this makes for a really refreshing salad at any time of the year, especially if you add some preserved lemons to help cut through the fat.

Pan-fried pork belly with courgettes, fennel & preserved lemon salad

Serves 6

1 kg (2 lb 4 oz) boneless piece pork belly, rind removed and fat scored
olive oil for frying
2 garlic cloves, bashed
few sprigs of lemon thyme
1 teaspoon fennel seeds
750 ml (25 fl oz) fresh chicken stock
3–4 courgettes (zucchini), sliced into ribbons
1 large fennel bulb, finely shredded
1 quantity of preserved lemons (page 143)
extra virgin olive oil, to drizzle
sea salt and freshly ground black pepper

Season the pork belly all over and cut into six pieces. Heat a layer of oil in a deep frying pan and brown the pork belly all over. Add the garlic, lemon thyme and fennel seeds. Cook for a minute more, then add the stock. Bring to the boil and simmer very gently, covered, for 45 minutes.

Toss the courgettes, fennel and preserved lemons together in a bowl. Drizzle with extra virgin olive oil and season. Serve the salad with the pork belly.

QUALITE EXTRA

Like English asparagus, I think the spring lamb we get here is some of the best in the world. It's also really good value if you buy something like a whole shoulder, during the season.

My friend Gloria from Mas Rabiol almost always uses milk-fed lamb, which comes from the farm next to her – you can't get fresher than that!

You can grill the shoulder on an open fire; the smoky flavour is a perfect match for the asparagus and the samphire.

Slow-cooked lamb shoulder with asparagus & samphire

Serves 6

3 sprigs of marjoram, leaves stripped and finely chopped
small bunch of finely chopped parsley
3 anchovies, finely chopped
3 garlic cloves, crushed
finely grated zest of 1 lemon
1 tablespoon capers, drained and rinsed
splash of sherry vinegar
4 tablespoons olive oil, plus extra to drizzle
1 large lamb shoulder (about 2 kg/4 lb 7 oz), boned
200 ml (7 fl oz) fino sherry
2 bunches of asparagus
200 g (7 oz) trimmed and washed samphire
sea salt and freshly ground black pepper

Preheat the oven to 200°C (400°F/Gas 6).

Mix together the herbs and anchovies with the garlic, lemon zest, capers and vinegar. Season well and add the olive oil to make a paste. Unroll the lamb and spread the mixture all over the inside. Loosely roll it up and tie with cook's string. Put the lamb in a roasting tin, drizzle with oil and season all over.

Roast for 20 minutes, then lower the oven temperature to 150°C (300°F/Gas 2). Pour in the sherry and add a splash of water, then cover with kitchen foil and cook for 2½–3 hours until really tender.

Cook the asparagus in boiling water for 1 minute. Add the samphire and cook for 30 seconds. Drain and refresh in cold water.

When the lamb is cooked, set the meat aside to rest. Skim the fat from the cooking juices and toss the asparagus and samphire through the juices. Slice the lamb and serve with the vegetables.

This recipe is from my dear friends Lara and Eduardo. I met them here in London, but they recently moved to Barcelona. They have been a great help in the research for this book.

I had never tried this recipe before, but had the chance on the day that we were on our photoshoot in L'Empordà. I couldn't wait to try it. Normally it is cooked with hen, not chicken.

This is a great dish for when your friends come over – it is ready to put in the oven and enjoy. Gracias to Lara and Eduardo!

Chicken cannelloni

Serves 6–8

olive oil for frying
200 g (7 oz) chicken breast, cut into pieces
150 g (5½ oz) minced (ground) beef
150 g (5½ oz) smoked lardons
100 g (3½ oz) white butifarra sausage, finely chopped
100 g (3½ oz) foie gras or chicken livers, cut into cubes
2 small onions, finely chopped
1 bay leaf
350 ml (12 fl oz) double (heavy) cream
50 ml (1¾ fl oz) dry sherry
10–12 fresh cannelloni or thin lasagne sheets
60 g (2 oz) grated Serrat (a mature cow's milk cheese from the Catalan Pyrenees) or any mature, hard manchego cheese
sea salt and freshly ground black pepper

for the béchamel sauce
1.7 litres (3 pints) fresh chicken stock
80 g (2¾ oz) unsalted butter
80 g (2¾ oz/⅔ cup) plain (all-purpose) flour
250 ml (8 fl oz) single (light) cream
pinch of nutmeg

Heat a layer of oil in a heavy-based pan and brown the meat (except for the foie gras) all over in batches, transferring to a bowl once browned.

Turn down the heat, add the onions to the pan and cook slowly until transparent. Stir in the bay leaf and plenty of seasoning. Cook for 1–2 minutes.

Add the foie gras and return the browned meat to the pan. Pour in the cream and cook to reduce for around 10 minutes. Add the sherry and cook for 2 minutes. Remove from the heat.

Mince everything (except for the cheese) in a food processor until you get a stuffing with a uniform texture. Place in a large piping bag and set aside.

To make the sauce, bring the stock to a simmer and keep it warm. Heat a heavy-based pan and melt the butter. Stir in the flour, mix well and cook for 1–2 minutes. Add the stock, little by little, stirring constantly. When smooth, add the cream, nutmeg and plenty of seasoning and simmer until lovely and thick. Set aside.

Preheat the grill (broiler) to medium high.

Place the pasta sheets on a board, pipe a good line of stuffing down the centre of each, then roll up the pasta to form cannelloni. You want a double layer of pasta, so if the sheets are too large, cut them to the right size with a sharp knife.

Spread a layer of béchamel in the bottom of an ovenproof dish and place the cannelloni on top, next to each other. Cover with the remaining béchamel and scatter with the grated cheese.

Place under the grill for around 10 minutes until golden brown and bubbling. Serve immediately.

If you go to Palafrugell, you must visit the market. It's a great place to go for all the food you'll need for the day or weekend ahead, and you'll inevitably end up buying many things you didn't go there for, just because there's so much choice. The farmers are very proud of what they've brought to market, so spend a little time chatting to them and they'll be delighted.

On the day we went, the ox cheek that was available was just stunning, so we made this dish for our lunch.

Slow-cooked ox cheek in spicy tomato sauce

Serves 6

4 tablespoons olive oil
1.5 kg (3 lb 5 oz) ox cheek in large chunks
2 tablespoons plain (all-purpose) flour, to dust
1 large onion, finely chopped
2 carrots, finely chopped
1 celery stalk, finely chopped
6 anchovies, chopped
2 teaspoons sweet smoked pimentón
2 teaspoons hot smoked pimentón
handful of thyme sprigs
300 ml (10 fl oz) red wine
2 × 400 g (14 oz) tins chopped tomatoes
150 ml (5 fl oz) chicken stock

Heat half the oil in a casserole dish (Dutch oven). Dust the ox cheek in the flour with plenty of seasoning, add to the dish and brown in batches. Set aside.

Heat the rest of the oil in the pan and fry the onion, carrot and celery for 10 minutes until softened. Add the anchovies and pimentón and cook for a minute. Then add the thyme and red wine and bubble until reduced by half.

Add the tomatoes and stock and bring to the boil. Simmer gently, covered, for 2 hours. Uncover and cook for a further 30 minutes – 1 hour, or until the ox cheek is really tender and the sauce reduced and thickened. Rest for 15 minutes, then serve with the chicory and pomegranate salad on page 153, if you like.

Fish

What can I say? Catalonia is obviously largely a coastal region, with some of the most beautiful little bays, beaches and rocky areas. But that's not all. There are rivers and even an area where saltwater meets fresh water. This diversity of water sources naturally produces a huge range of incredible seafood – we're so lucky.

The stunning colours of nature and light in Catalonia equate to an extraordinary variety of colours in the region's fish – really wow. We have a wonderful selection of fish here in the UK too – I'm always amazed by what my fishmonger brings to the restaurant. So make your fishmonger your friend and give some of these recipes a go.

I first encountered Maruja and her husband Florian thanks to Josep Cuní, a great Catalan journalist I met in London, who was kind enough to show us around Begur, a small village on the Costa Brava – if you haven't been, go!

Maruja reminds me a lot of my mum Isabel; a strong woman who, even after a really long day, still enjoys preparing food for her guests, always with fresh ingredients and with a mother's love. *Suquet* simply means 'fish stew' in Catalan.

Suquet

Serves 6–8

100 ml (3½ fl oz) olive oil
1 large onion, finely chopped
2 garlic cloves, crushed
2 × 400 g (14 oz) tins chopped tomatoes
1 litre (34 fl oz) fresh fish stock
600 g (1 lb 5 oz) new potatoes
600 g (1 lb 5 oz) mix of monkfish, turbot and bream in large pieces
plain (all-purpose) flour, to dust
sea salt and freshly ground black pepper

for the picada
100 ml (3½ fl oz) olive oil
2 garlic cloves, crushed
2 small onions, chopped
1 slice white sourdough or bread
2 squares dark chocolate, grated
20 g (¾ oz) blanched almonds
handful of parsley

Heat 75 ml (2½ fl oz) of the oil in a large pan, add the onion and gently fry for 15 minutes until softened. Add the garlic, fry for a couple of minutes, then add the tomatoes and plenty of seasoning. Simmer gently for 30–45 minutes until the mixture is really thick but not dry.

Meanwhile, make the picada. Heat a little of the oil in a pan and gently fry the garlic and onions until soft. Remove from the pan and set aside. Heat a little more oil and fry the bread until golden but not crunchy. Add to the onions and garlic with the rest of the ingredients and whiz in a food processor or mash in a pestle and mortar, with enough of the oil to make a paste. Set aside.

Add the stock to the reduced tomato mixture and bring to a simmer. Insert the tip of a sharp knife into the potatoes and twist to crack them open (instead of slicing). Add to the pan and cook for 15 minutes until starting to soften.

While the potatoes are cooking, heat the remaining oil in a non-stick pan. Dust the fish in flour and fry for a minute or two until lightly golden on both sides. Set aside.

Once the potatoes are nearly cooked, add the picada to the sauce and stir well. Nestle the fish into the pan and cook for a further 4–5 minutes until the sauce is thickened and the fish just cooked (when the fish is opaque and a knife inserted into it goes in easily). Serve with lots of crusty bread.

This is my idea of the perfect comfort food. You have to eat it with your hands – getting a bit messy is part of it.

I've made some changes to the traditional recipe, which usually has lots more sauce and is served in a bowl rather than on toast. The sardines are also usually grilled, not fried.

I also used potatoes to thicken the sauce, rather than *picada*, as I think it makes it all the more comforting.

Sardines on toast with suquet

Serves 4

50 ml (1¾ fl oz) olive oil
2 large onions, finely chopped
1 green (bell) pepper, finely chopped
1 tablespoon pimentón
500 g (1 lb 2 oz) small waxy potatoes
1 dried choricero pepper
300 ml (10 fl oz) fresh fish stock
sea salt and freshly ground black pepper

for the sardines
4 small fresh sardines, filleted
1 garlic clove, finely sliced
zest of 1 lemon and a squeeze of juice
2 tablespoons finely chopped parsley
olive oil for deep-frying
3 tablespoons plain (all-purpose) flour, seasoned with salt and pepper
1 free-range egg, beaten
4 slices sourdough, toasted
extra virgin olive oil, to drizzle

Put the sardines in a dish with the garlic, lemon zest and juice and parsley. Set aside to marinate while you make the suquet.

Heat the olive oil in a pan and gently fry the onions and pepper for 20 minutes until really softened. Add the pimentón and cook for a minute. Insert the tip of a sharp knife into the potatoes and twist to crack them open (instead of slicing). Add them to the pan with the choricero pepper, stock and plenty of seasoning. Cover and simmer gently for 40 minutes until the potatoes are tender and the sauce thick.

In a small, deep pan, heat the olive oil for deep-frying to 180°C (350°F) – or until a cube of bread browns in 20 seconds. Remove the sardines from the marinade and pat dry with kitchen paper. Dip in the seasoned flour, then in the beaten egg. Carefully drop into the oil and fry for just a minute or two until golden and crisp. Remove with a slotted spoon and drain on kitchen paper.

Spoon the suquet onto the toasted sourdough, top with the fried sardines and drizzle with extra virgin olive oil to finish.

Arroz negro is a very popular and really delicious recipe, normally made with squid ink, squid and prawns (shrimp), topped off with some alioli.

This recipe is a bit different because we use the onions to give the rice its colour, cooking them down for a long time. A few people from Girona told me that this is the original recipe. I don't know how true this is, but it is extremely good.

I love squid ink, but this way, you won't stain your lips black!

Arroz negro with cuttlefish & butifarra

Serves 4

70 ml (2½ fl oz) olive oil
150 g (5½ oz) black butifarra sausage, chopped
350 g (12 oz) fresh cuttlefish, cleaned and finely chopped
4 large onions, finely chopped
250 g (9 oz/1 cup) bomba rice or other short-grain rice
1 litre (34 fl oz) fresh fish stock
sea salt and freshly ground black pepper

Heat the olive oil in a pan and fry the meat and fish until browned all over. Scoop out with a slotted spoon and set aside.

Add the onions to the pan with some seasoning and cook very, very gently for 2–3 hours, until really soft and dark brown. If they look as though they will catch, add a tiny splash of water.

Return the meat and fish to the pan and add the rice and stock. Bring to the boil and simmer for 15 minutes, stirring occasionally until the stock is absorbed and the rice just cooked. Serve straightaway.

This recipe comes from Head Chef Aleix at my restaurant Pizarro – he's a great Catalan chef and has given me lots of ideas for this book.

People would normally use salted cod in Catalonia, but we use fresh cod and cure it ourselves with plenty of good sea salt. Don't use table salt as it contains additives and has a different flavour.

Bacallà a la llauna, spinach & piquillo peppers

Serves 6

1.2 kg (2 lb 10 oz) chunky cod loin, skin left on
750 g (1 lb 10 oz/2½ cups) coarse sea salt
2–3 tablespoons plain (all-purpose) flour
250 ml (8 fl oz) light olive oil
4 garlic cloves, finely sliced
2 teaspoons pimentón
50 ml (1¾ fl oz) sherry vinegar
3 piquillo peppers, drained, opened out and halved
1 tablespoon olive oil
120 g (4 oz) raisins
3 tablespoons pine nuts
500 g (1 lb 2 oz) baby spinach

Put the cod in a plastic container, cover completely with the salt and set aside for 20–30 minutes. Rinse and dry, then cut into six pieces and dust all over with flour.

Preheat the oven to 180°C (350°F/Gas 4).

Heat the light olive oil in an ovenproof pan – not too hot – and add the fish. Cook on the stovetop for 5 minutes, turning halfway through, until lightly golden. Remove with a slotted spoon onto a plate lined with kitchen paper.

Add the garlic to the oil and fry gently for a minute. Add the pimentón and vinegar. Return the fish to the pan and lay the piquillo peppers on top. Put in the oven for 5–6 minutes until the fish is just cooked (when it is just opaque and a thin knife inserts without resistance).

Meanwhile, heat the olive oil in a pan and fry the raisins and pine nuts until the pine nuts are starting to turn golden. Add the spinach and quickly sauté until just beginning to wilt. Divide between six warmed plates, top each with a piece of fish and pepper and spoon over the sauce. Serve with bread.

Sunday is *vermut* – vermouth – day in Catalonia, and people typically have a can or tin of seafood or fish with their drinks. These might be cockles, sardines or, of course, *mejillones en escabeche*, which they serve in their own tins with a big plate of crisps.

Here is my recipe for mejillones en escabeche, which is easy, yummy and ideal for every day of the week.

Mussels in escabeche

Serves 4

2 tablespoons olive oil
1 small onion, finely chopped
1 small carrot, finely sliced
1 celery stalks, finely sliced
1 teaspoon pimentón
1 garlic clove, finely sliced
2–3 sprigs of fresh thyme
1 fresh bay leaf
75 ml (2½ fl oz) vermouth vinegar
200 ml (7 fl oz) white wine
150 ml (5 fl oz) fresh shellfish stock
1 kg (2 lb 4 oz) fresh mussels, cleaned
sea salt and freshly ground black pepper

Heat the oil in a pan and add the vegetables. Cook for 15 minutes until very tender, then add the pimentón, garlic and herbs and cook for a minute or two more. Add the vinegar and bubble for a minute before adding the wine and stock. Season well, cover and cook gently for 40 minutes. At this point you can set the escabeche aside until you are ready to cook the mussels – the flavour will intensify if left to rest for a few hours.

When ready to serve, reheat the escabeche. Put a large pan on a high heat. When really hot, add the mussels and a splash of water, cover and cook for 1–2 minutes until they are just opened and cooked (discard any mussels that stay shut).

Tip into a large bowl, spoon over the escabeche and serve.

La Tancada is a restaurant in Amposta, which also has facilities for camping, if you fancy it. It's part of the province of Tarragona, a gorgeous part of the country.

I go there for the *xapadillo*, which on my research trip was one of the best things I tried. Xapadillo is deep-fried eel, which might not sound very exciting but, with its golden colour and crispy texture, and the eel caught just a few metres from the restaurant, what could be better?

Xapadillo

Serves 2–4

1 fresh eel or 2 smaller – 500 g (1 lb 2 oz)
600 g (1 lb 5 oz) coarse sea salt
pared zest and juice of 1 orange
olive oil for deep-frying

Cut the head off the eel, split it in half lengthways and clean (you can ask your fishmonger to do this for you). Put it in a plastic container and mix with the salt, orange zest, then juice and leave to cure for 5 hours.

Remove the eel from the container, wash it and pat it dry with kitchen paper. Hang it up to dry in the fridge on a wine rack (or other hanging space, such as some balanced bamboo skewers) for 24 hours.

Heat a small, deep pan of olive oil to 180°C (350°F) – or until a cube of bread browns in 20 seconds. Cut the eel into pieces and plunge into the hot oil. Fry for 2–3 minutes until crispy and golden and cooked.
Eat straightaway.

I'm a big fan of salt cod, and here is one of my favourite salads using this great ingredient.

Everyone seems to make their bacalao by de-salting the cod in water for about 24 hours, but I love it so much that I just take the salty skin off straightaway and break into small pieces to clean in water for about 20 minutes. If you prefer bacalao less salty, then just soak it for a bit longer and change the water more often.

Xató sauce is very similar to romesco; remember not to make the sauce too salty, as you'll get this from the fish anyway.

Xató

Serves 4

1 large tomato, halved
15 g (½ oz) Marcona almonds
15 g (½ oz) blanched hazelnuts
200 ml (7 fl oz) olive oil for frying
5 garlic cloves, peeled
40 g (1½ oz) slightly stale white bread, torn into pieces
1 tablespoon sherry vinegar
400 g (14 oz) salt cod, broken into pieces and soaked in cold water for 20 minutes or overnight (change the water a couple of times if you can), depending on how salty you like it
1 frisée lettuce, washed and leaves torn
100 g (3½ oz) unpitted black olives
sea salt and freshly ground black pepper

Cook the tomato under a hot grill (broiler) until really tender.

Meanwhile, toast the nuts in a dry pan until starting to turn golden. Set aside.

Heat the oil in the pan over a low heat and add the garlic. Fry for a few minutes until golden and tender, then add the bread and fry together until the bread also turns golden. Add the nuts to the pan and cook for a little longer, then tip into a food processor. Add the tomato (discard the skin) and vinegar, whiz and season to taste.

Drain the salt cod and pat dry. Arrange the lettuce leaves on a plate, scatter with the salt cod pieces, drizzle with the xató sauce and top with the black olives.

I need to have razor clams whenever I see them on the menu! Served here with jamón ibérico and a glass of cava – dreamy.

In this recipe I clean the clams by taking out the foot and stomach and slicing them to mix with the vinaigrette. I do love them just open – put on the plancha and eat the whole thing in one go.

Razor clams with jamón & cava vinaigrette

Serves 4

24 small fresh razor clams
olive oil for frying
75 g (2½ oz) jamón, finely chopped
1 small shallot, finely chopped
handful of chopped parsley
small bunch of finely chopped chives
2 tablespoons cava
good squeeze of lemon juice
4 tablespoons extra virgin olive oil
sea salt and freshly ground black pepper

Put a large pan with a lid over a high heat. Rinse the razor clams thoroughly under cold running water. Add to the pan with a splash of water and cover with the lid. Cook, shaking the pan, for 30 seconds until the clams have just opened (discard any that stay shut).

Remove the meat from the shells. With a sharp knife cut away the foot/digger – which is the bulbous dark bit at one end – and remove the central stomach sack and intestinal tract, so you are left only with the sweet, firm white meat.

Meanwhile, heat a little olive oil in a frying pan and fry the jamón until crispy. Remove with a slotted spoon and set aside, leaving the fat in the pan.

Mix the shallot and herbs with the cava and lemon juice and season well. Whisk in the extra virgin olive oil.

Put the frying pan back on the heat and fry the clams in the jamón fat until they have just finished cooking. Serve scattered with the jamón and drizzled with the dressing.

L'Escala is a beautiful place on the Costa Brava, and has always been famous for its fishing industry. The anchovies here are well known for braving the cold waters.

Traditionally, the men would go out to fish and the women would then prepare, cook and cure the fish.

Nowadays, anchovies come already cleaned, boned and in oil, or you can find them salted in small jars – these you have to clean yourself, which is my favourite way to buy them – wonderful!

Anchovies de L'Escala ensalada

Serves 4

5–6 tablespoons plain yoghurt
2 teaspoons chopped marjoram
finely grated zest of ½ lemon
handful of torn frisée lettuce leaves
12–16 anchovy fillets
1 ripe tomato, peeled, deseeded and chopped
extra virgin olive oil, to drizzle
4 small slices sourdough, toasted
sea salt and freshly ground black pepper

Mix the yoghurt with the marjoram and lemon zest and season to taste.

Toss the lettuce leaves with the anchovies, chopped tomato and a drizzle of extra virgin olive oil.

Spoon the yoghurt mixture onto the toasts and pile with the anchovy and tomato salad and serve.

I've brought a little sweetness to this recipe by adding some caramelised onions. You could also pan-fry some black butifarra and add it at the end, for another *mar y montaña* recipe.

We were cooking for all the team at Empordá and I couldn't resist adding some beautiful rosemary flowers to the dish, not only for the colour but for the taste too.

Sautéed baby squid with broad beans & mint

Serves 4

50 ml (1¾ fl oz) olive oil, plus extra for frying
50 g (1¾ oz) unsalted butter
2 large onions, very finely sliced
500 g (1 lb 2 oz) fresh baby squid, cleaned
300 g (10½ oz) baby broad (fava) beans
150 ml (5 fl oz) light fresh fish stock
2 tablespoons chopped mint
rosemary flowers, to sprinkle (optional)

Heat the olive oil and butter in a pan and, when foaming, add the onions. Cook slowly for 10 minutes, then cover with a lid and cook for 45–50 minutes until the onions are really sticky and caramelised.

When the onions are nearly cooked, heat a layer of oil in a clean pan over a really high heat. Fry the baby squid for a couple of minutes until almost cooked and slightly charred. Add the squid to the onions with the broad beans and stock and simmer for a few minutes until the beans and squid are tender. Add the mint and rosemary flowers, if using. Serve straightaway.

Pasta dishes have been a big part of Catalan cuisine since the seventeenth century, and some of the old recipes are still really well known today, such as the cannelloni on page 60 or *Fideuà* or *Sopa de galets*, which is typically served at Christmas. *Galets* are big pasta shells, and the soup has meatballs in it as well.

I tried something similar to this recipe at a restaurant in the old shipyard area of Barceloneta. The restaurant is called Suquet de l'Almirall – it's so worth heading down there to try it. That, and the paella Denominación Origen (D.O.) Barceloneta.

Rigatoni with prawns & mussels

Serves 4

350 g (12 oz) dried rigatoni
500 g (1 lb 2 oz) fresh mussels, cleaned
2 tablespoons olive oil
50 g (1¾ oz) butter
1 banana shallot (eschalion), finely chopped
½ garlic clove, crushed
16 large raw prawns (shrimp), peeled and tails left on
300 ml (10 fl oz) fresh shellfish stock
100 ml (3½ fl oz) double (heavy) cream
squeeze of lemon juice
1 tablespoon snipped chives

Bring a pan of salted water to the boil and cook the rigatoni for 10–12 minutes until just tender.

Meanwhile, put a large pan over a high heat. When really hot, add the mussels with a splash of water, cover with a lid and steam until just opened. Drain (discard any that stay shut) and then pick all the meat from the shells.

In another pan, heat the oil and butter and fry the shallot for 10 minutes until tender. Add the garlic and prawns and fry until the prawns are pink all over. Remove the prawns and set aside.

Add the stock and cream to the pan you fried the prawns in. Simmer until thickened, then add a squeeze of lemon juice. Drain the pasta and add to the sauce with the fish and chives. Serve straightaway.

As you may know, I'm a huge fan of big pots or large pieces of meat or fish, cooked simply. This monkfish recipe looks very impressive when you put it on the table. Easy for a party as you don't need to do much – just enjoy yourself.

Roast monkfish tail with lemon thyme salsa

Serves 4–6

4 banana shallots (eschalions), peeled and cut into wedges
1 bulb garlic, cloves separated
500 g (1 lb 2 oz) potatoes, chopped
500 g (1 lb 2 oz) small vine tomatoes, halved
12–14 caper berries
few sprigs of lemon thyme
olive oil
2 kg (4 lb 7 oz) whole bone in monkfish tail, skinned
100 ml (3½ fl oz) white wine
sea salt and freshly ground black pepper

for the salsa

4 sprigs of lemon thyme, leaves stripped
large handful of chopped parsley
finely grated zest and juice of 1 lemon
1 red chilli, finely chopped
1 bulb garlic, roasted until soft
120 ml (4 fl oz) extra virgin olive oil

Preheat the oven to 200°C (400°F/Gas 6).

Toss the shallots, garlic, potatoes, tomatoes, caper berries and lemon thyme together in a roasting tin with a good drizzle of olive oil and plenty of seasoning.

Rub the monkfish with oil, season well and place on top of the vegetables. Roast in the oven for 20 minutes, then add the wine and roast for a further 20–25 minutes until the fish is just cooked and the vegetables are really tender.

Meanwhile, make the salsa. In a small food processor blitz together the herbs, lemon zest and juice, and chilli. When the fish is cooked, squeeze the roasted garlic flesh into the salsa. Whiz again with enough extra virgin olive oil to loosen. Serve the fish and vegetables with the salsa to drizzle over.

Seeing red mullet on the fish counter, or at the port, makes me really happy. It's a gorgeous fish with stunning flavour, the eyes saying 'buy me and cook me'!

The idea for this recipe came to me after I'd tried something at my dear friend Rick Stein's restaurant in Padstow – the red mullet was stuffed with white crab meat. Delicious.

I've made this recipe a bit differently to reflect Catalan ingredients, and I think it works brilliantly.

Red mullet stuffed with anchovies, olives & capers

Serves 4

6 salted anchovies
75 g (2½ oz) black olives
1 garlic clove
1 tablespoon capers, drained and rinsed
handful of parsley, torn
finely grated zest of 1 lemon
1 hard-boiled free-range egg yolk
1–2 tablespoons olive oil, plus extra for frying
4 red mullet, filleted
1 kg (2 lb 4 oz) ripe heirloom tomatoes, sliced
handful of tarragon stalks, leaves stripped
extra virgin olive oil

In a small food processor or using a heavy pestle and mortar, blitz the anchovies, olives, garlic, capers, parsley, lemon zest and egg yolk until you have a rough paste. Add enough olive oil to loosen.

Put four of the red mullet fillets skin side down on a board. Spread them with the anchovy mixture, then put a second fillet, skin side up, on top to make a sandwich. Tie up with some cook's string.

In a bowl, mix the tomatoes with the tarragon and a good glug of extra virgin olive oil.

Heat a little oil in a pan and fry the fish for 1–2 minutes on each side until just cooked and golden. Serve the mullet sandwiches with the tomato salad.

todo

va mejor

Cola

		PEIX	
PAN TOSTADO	1'80	CAL. ROMANA	6'20
BOMBA	2'00	ARENGUE	2'50
MORCILLAS	3'50	SARDINAS	5'50
~~XAMPINYONS~~	—	BARAT	6'00
BACON	1'40	CALAMAR	6'[illegible]
HABAS	2'20	PULPO	4'00
BUTIFARRA	3'50	RECORTES PULPO	4'00
CHORIZO	3'50	BACALAO	6'00
CAP i POTA	4'00	ESCABECHE	5'00
AMANIDA	2'40	ESQUEIXADA	4'50
JUDIAS	[illegible]	GAMBES	1[illegible]'00
GARBANZOS	[illegible]	ESCAMARLA	12'00
ENSALADILLA	3'00	BUNYOLS BAC.	3'60
[illegible]	3'[illegible]	[illegible]	3'70

I've had different versions of this recipe in several places – in Atrio in Cáceres and at La Tancada too. At Atrio, they finish it with caviar and at La Tancada with olive oil, cherry tomatoes and local flowers. Both different, both fantastic. This is an impressive dish to try – and your guests will be pleased you did!

One of the chefs I came across, Xavi, brought this to the menu. He's a young and talented chef who creates great combinations, textures and flavours.

Gambas carpaccio

Serves 2

handful of basil leaves
170 ml (6 fl oz) extra virgin olive oil
100 g (3½ oz) mixed cherry tomatoes, peeled
300 g (10½ oz) large raw prawns (shrimp), peeled and deveined
edible flowers to garnish
sea salt and freshly ground black pepper

Blanch the basil leaves in boiling water for 2 seconds, then rinse under cold water and drain on kitchen paper. Put into a small food processor with 70 ml (2½ fl oz) of the exra virgin olive oil and blitz together. Set aside.

Toss the peeled cherry tomatoes in the rest of the oil with plenty of seasoning. Leave to marinate for 30 minutes to 1 hour.

Butterfly the prawns using a very sharp knife, then slice them very thinly on the diagonal to give the largest surface area, similar to slicing gravadlax or smoked salmon.

Arrange the prawns on a plate. Remove the tomatoes from the oil, halve and dot over the prawns. Scatter with the edible flowers and drizzle with the basil oil. Finally, sprinkle with sea salt and serve.

When you see a tray of these beauties coming to your table, I promise you'll be happy.

In the UK we have the most amazing langoustines from Scotland; just ask your fishmonger for them.

Don't forget to mop the juices from the tray – the lemon will help to keep the juices and add a bit of the acidity.

Roast langoustines

Serves 4

36 live langoustines
juice of 1 lemon
olive oil

Preheat the oven to 200°c (400°F/Gas 6). Take each langoustine and slice it in half down the middle in one quick, clean cut. Squeeze a little lemon juice over the flesh.

Put the langoustines on a baking tray, cut side up, and drizzle with olive oil. Roast quickly for 4–5 minutes, then serve straightaway with some bread to mop up the juices.

A traditional recipe from the area known as Tierras del Ebro, I think it's the perfect food to enjoy with some friends, sitting outside on a sunny day. This is right up my street.

Grill the vegetables and fish and then put on a piece of crusty bread. Oh yes, bring me a cold beer!

Clotxa

Serves 4

350 g (12 oz) cherry tomatoes
170 g (6 oz) shallots, peeled
1 bulb garlic, cloves separated
1 leek, sliced
3–4 sprigs of thyme, leaves stripped
olive oil
400 g (14 oz) round loaf of white bread
3–4 fresh sardines, filleted
sea salt and freshly ground black pepper

Preheat the oven to 200°C (400°F/Gas 6).

Put the tomatoes, shallots, garlic, leek and thyme in a roasting tin and drizzle with olive oil. Season well and roast for 30–40 minutes, turning occasionally, until tender and soft.

Slice the top off the loaf and hollow out all the bread from the centre (you can keep this for eating with the dish later if you like).

When the vegetables are nearly cooked, heat a little oil in a pan and fry the sardines for a couple of minutes on each side until golden and cooked.

Spoon the roasted vegetables and all the juices into the hollowed-out loaf and arrange the fish on top. Serve straightaway with lots of extra bread to mop up the juices.

I love going on *Saturday Kitchen* – it's such a buzz and an opportunity to cook with some wonderful chefs. I was on the show with the brilliant Andi Oliver a few months ago, and she cooked a whole cauliflower with turmeric and Stilton cream, which was so delicious I've been looking at what I could do with a whole roasted cauliflower. Here it is! Remember not to waste the leaves; just trim them from the cauliflower, fry in a little butter and garlic and serve on the side.

Whole roasted cauliflower with anchovy sauce

Serves 4–6

1 whole large cauliflower
olive oil
2 banana shallots (eschalions), finely chopped
3 garlic cloves, finely sliced
good pinch of dried chilli flakes
8 salted anchovies, finely chopped
600 g (1 lb 5 oz) fresh tomatoes, finely chopped
75 ml (2½ fl oz) fresh vegetable stock
100 ml (3½ fl oz) double (heavy) cream
50 g (1¾ oz) unsalted butter
sea salt and freshly ground black pepper

Preheat the oven to 200°C (400°F/Gas 6).

Remove the leaves from the cauliflower and set aside to use later. Bring a large pan of salted water to the boil and blanch the cauliflower for 4–5 minutes. Drain well.

Put the cauliflower in a roasting tin and drizzle all over with olive oil. Season well and roast for 40–50 minutes until it is tender and golden.

Meanwhile, make the sauce. Add a little oil to a pan and gently fry the shallots for 10 minutes until softened. Add half of the garlic and the chilli flakes and cook for a minute more. Add the anchovies and let them dissolve, then add the tomatoes and stock.

Season and cook for 10–15 minutes until the tomatoes have broken down. Add the cream and bubble for a minute more.

Heat the butter in a separate pan with the rest of the garlic and fry the cauliflower leaves with plenty of seasoning. Serve the cauliflower with the buttery leaves and the anchovy sauce spooned over the top.

I think this is one of the dishes that I cook the most at home. It's super-simple and, as ever with fish, it's quick to cook so is great if you're hungry and want to eat in a hurry.

Ask your fishmonger to source the big wild fish for you if they can, as this will work best.

The orange and red onion salad is a perfect match for this fish, but it's also great to enjoy with any grilled meat or fish.

Salt-baked sea bream with orange & pickled red onion salad

Serves 4

2 free-range egg whites
250 g (9 oz/¾ cup) coarse sea salt
10 sprigs of thyme, leaves stripped
4 bay leaves
2 whole sea bream (about 600–700 g/1 lb 5 oz–1 lb 9 oz each), gutted

for the salad

2 red onions, cut into thin wedges
2 teaspoons coriander seeds
100 ml (3½ fl oz) white wine vinegar
50 ml (1¾ fl oz) sherry vinegar
60 g (2 oz/¼ cup) caster (superfine) sugar
2 oranges, peeled and sliced
handful of parsley, leaves stripped
1 head radicchio, leaves torn
extra virgin olive oil, to drizzle

Preheat the oven to 180°C (350°F/Gas 4).

For the salad, put the onions in a bowl with the coriander seeds. In a small pan heat the vinegars, sugar and 100 ml (3½ fl oz) of water until the sugar melts. Then pour the hot liquid over the onions. Leave to marinate while you cook the fish.

Beat the egg whites and mix with the salt, thyme and bay leaves. Put two layers of the salt mixture on a baking tray about the same size as the fish. Place the fish on top of the salt and cover with the remaining mixture. Pat the fish down so they are completely covered. Bake for 25–30 minutes until the salt has hardened. Let the fish rest while you finish the salad.

Drain the onion and toss with the orange slices, parsley and radicchio. Drizzle with lots of extra virgin olive oil. Crack open the fish and serve with the salad.

All across Delta del Ebro you will find great restaurants where you can enjoy the local rice speciality, cooked with other local ingredients. This is my lobster rice recipe, with a little help from Ca'l Faiges … the flavour of their lobster is to die for.

If you are lucky enough to go there, don't order one per person – the portion sizes are really generous! And remember to ask for the *ortiguillas* (anemones) too. They're simply deep-fried – you won't regret ordering them.

Lobster rice

Serves 6-8

2 live lobsters (about 700 g/ 1 lb 9 oz each)
500 ml (17 fl oz) fresh shellfish stock
500 ml (17 fl oz) fresh chicken stock
60 ml (2 fl oz) olive oil
2 large onions, finely chopped
4 garlic cloves, sliced
300 g (10½ oz/1⅓ cups) bomba or other short-grain rice
200 ml (7 fl oz) white wine
600 g (1 lb 5 oz) fresh tomatoes, finely chopped
good pinch of saffron threads
500 g (1 lb 2 oz) hake, cut into chunks
500 g (1 lb 2 oz) fresh clams, cleaned
sea salt and freshly ground black pepper

With a sharp, heavy knife, cut the lobsters in half down the middle in one swift movement. Remove the stomach and discard. Remove the claws and crack them with the back of a knife or a rolling pin. Remove the small legs.

Combine the stocks in a pan and heat until steaming.

Heat the oil in a very large pan. Gently fry the onions for 10 minutes until softened. Add the garlic and rice and fry for a minute until the rice is toasted. Add the wine and tomatoes and cook, stirring, until the wine is absorbed, then add the saffron threads.

Pour 750 ml (25 fl oz) of the hot stock into the rice, stir well and season to taste. Nestle the lobsters into the rice, and cook gently, without stirring, for 15 minutes. Add the hake and cook for a further 3–5 minutes, then add the clams and a further splash (150–200 ml/5–7 fl oz) of stock. Cover and cook for 1–2 minutes until the clams are open (discard any that stay shut).

Serve straightaway with lots of bread.

Florian from Begur made me this dish with his catch of the day. He put the calamari on the plancha, and I remember we just sat in his garden on that glorious spring day and ate the lot! Such wonderful hospitality. The picture opposite is of Florian's recipe – it tasted as incredible as it looks!

I've added a few more ingredients here and I think they're a match made in heaven.

Marinated grilled squid

Serves 4

4 small fresh squid, cleaned and cut into large strips
100 ml (3½ fl oz) olive oil
1 garlic clove, bashed
few sprigs of thyme or rosemary
flaky sea salt
extra virgin olive oil, to drizzle
lemon wedges, to serve

Put the squid in a container with the oil, garlic and herbs and leave to marinate for a few hours.

Heat a plancha or heavy-based pan until it is very hot. Cook the squid for 1–2 minutes on each side until curled up and golden.

Season to taste with sea salt and serve with a drizzle of extra virgin olive oil and lemon wedges to squeeze over.

The best clams in La Boquería market in Barcelona can be found at Bar Pinotxo. They travel from the fishmonger straight to the plancha where they meet some olive oil. The best way to enjoy these is with a glass of cava. And don't forget some bread for those juices.

Clams 'a la plancha' with olive oil

Serves 4

1 kg (2 lb 4 oz) large fresh clams, cleaned
flaky sea salt
extra virgin olive oil, to drizzle

Heat a plancha or heavy-based pan until very hot. Add the clams in a single layer and cook, turning once, for 1–2 minutes until they are opened (discard any that stay shut). Spoon into a large bowl, season to taste and drizzle with plenty of extra virgin olive oil. Serve straightaway with lots of bread to soak up the juices.

Vegetables

Some of my best friends are ... vegetarians! Although I'm not, that doesn't stop me appreciating and enjoying the wonderful world of vegetables. I especially like the first-class vegetables that grow in Catalonia. Being from a farming family, I grew up understanding the love and pleasure, but also the hard work, that goes into developing a vegetable garden.

Sometimes, if the ingredients are really great, fresh, and prepared and seasoned well, I just love to eat a vegetable dish on its own, letting the flavours speak for themselves. Raw or cooked, eaten on their own or as an accompaniment to a main dish, vegetables are so versatile that it's worth getting creative.

Cooking and enjoying a range of vegetables reminds me of listening to an orchestra – each has its own distinct character and flavour but, when prepared in harmony with others, can be an out-of-this-world food experience.

Priorat is the most beautiful area, and after a visit to Cellers de Scala Dei winery, we went for lunch at an amazing place – a small restaurant called El Rebost de la Cartoixa. I love this kind of restaurant – the welcome when you arrive, the retro look, paper tablecloths and, most importantly, the incredible smell of cooking.

I love too that the whole family is involved, with the mother in the kitchen, the father on the floor and daughters helping them at the weekend.

I had *escalivada*, which was just wonderful, with a smoky aroma and flavours coming from the charcoal, which is where the name originates from.

Escalivada is traditionally made with aubergines (eggplants) and red (bell) peppers; some say onions as well. El Rebost de la Cartoixa serve it with potatoes, onions, artichokes and asparagus, all cooked on the grill (broiler). Maybe not very traditional, but still delicious!

Escalivada

Serves 6

2 red (bell) peppers
2 medium potatoes
1 onion, left whole with skin on
2 aubergines (eggplants)
1 bulb garlic, cloves separated
4 ripe tomatoes
olive oil
2 globe artichokes
extra virgin olive oil, to drizzle
juice of 1 lemon
sea salt and freshly ground black pepper

Heat the grill (broiler) as high as it will go and blacken the peppers under it. Then pop them into a plastic bag to steam and loosen the skins.

Preheat the oven to 180°C (350°F/Gas 4).

Wrap the potatoes and onion in kitchen foil and put them in the oven to steam and cook for about 45–60 minutes, depending on size. Make a slit down each aubergine and stuff with a few garlic cloves. Put them in a roasting tin with the tomatoes, drizzle with olive oil and cook for 1 hour, removing the tomatoes after 30 minutes.

Cook the artichokes in a steamer for 20–30 minutes until they are really tender.

Remove the skins from the peppers, then halve them, remove the seeds and cut into strips. Peel the onion and cut into quarters. Thickly slice the potatoes. Allow the aubergines to cool a little, then peel and cut into strips.

Squeeze the garlic cloves from their skins. Arrange all the cooked vegetables and garlic on a platter, season with plenty of sea salt and black pepper and drizzle with lots of extra virgin olive oil and lemon juice. Serve warm or at room temperature.

You can find *cocas* of all kinds – sweet, savoury, very simple, very complicated – and all of them are great in my opinion. They are a sort of tongue-shaped 'pizza'.

This recipe is perfect if you fancy something vegetarian, but feel free to include some anchovies, which is one of my favourite additions. You could just change the toppings as you please, but do try to stick to some Catalonian flavours.

Vegetarian coca

Serves 6

12 g (½ oz) fresh yeast or 7 g (¼ oz) sachet fast-action dried yeast
330 ml (11¼ fl oz) lukewarm water
pinch of sugar
500 g (1 lb 2 oz/4 cups) plain (all-purpose) flour, plus extra to dust
10 g (½ oz) fine sea salt
1 tablespoon extra virgin olive oil
fine polenta, to dust

for the topping

1 small, firm pumpkin (squash), cut into small wedges
2 red onions, cut into wedges
olive oil
sea salt
few sprigs of thyme (or some sage leaves)
150 g (5½ oz) chestnuts

Cream the yeast in a bowl with a little of the water and a pinch of sugar. When smooth, add three-quarters of the remaining water and leave to stand, covered, for 30 minutes until the mixture starts to bubble.

Sift the flour and salt into the bowl of a stand mixer. Add the yeast water and olive oil and knead with the dough hook for 5 minutes on a low speed, adding more of the water if it looks a little dry. Leave to stand for 10 minutes, then knead again for 5 minutes until smooth and elastic. Cover and stand for 1 hour or until doubled in size.

Meanwhile, preheat the oven to 200°C (400°F/Gas 6). Put the pumpkin and onions in a roasting tin, drizzle with oil and season to taste with salt and the sage leaves. Roast for 30 minutes until the pumpkin is starting to become golden and tender. Remove from the oven.

Divide the dough into six equal portions, then roll out on a lightly floured surface into 30 cm (12 in) tongue-like shapes. Sprinkle two baking trays with a little polenta, place the dough pieces on top, cover with a clean dish towel and stand in a warm place for 15 minutes.

Heat the oven as high as it will go. Brush the dough bases lightly with olive oil and sprinkle with sea salt. Toss the chestnuts with the pumpkin and onions and divide between the breads, leaving a 2 cm (¾ in) border around the edge. Bake for 10–12 minutes, or until the bases are golden and crisp. Serve immediately.

Normally I would make this recipe with cuttlefish, ceps and artichokes. However, the ceps and artichoke are a delicious combination, and make this dish something that is particularly enjoyable for my vegetarian friends – just subtitute the chicken stock with vegetable stock to make it vegetarian. If you fancy adding some meat, finely slice some pancetta Ibérica, and add it at the end of cooking so it melts – it's just heaven on a plate!

Rice with ceps & artichokes

Serves 6–8

100 ml (3½ fl oz) olive oil for frying
2 onions, finely chopped
4 garlic cloves, crushed
400 g (14 oz/generous 1¾ cups) bomba rice or other short-grain rice
250 ml (8 fl oz) dry white wine
500 ml (17 fl oz) porcini stock
500 ml (17 fl oz) fresh chicken stock
10 baby artichokes, cleaned
200 g (7 oz) fresh ceps, sliced

Heat a very large pan or paella pan over a low heat and add 75 ml (2½ fl oz) of the oil. Gently fry the onion for 15 minutes until really soft. Add the garlic and rice and stir well to toast the grains for a minute or two.

Heat the wine and stocks in a pan, then pour into the rice. Season to taste and stir, then push the baby artichokes into the rice and leave to cook without stirring over a low heat for 20 minutes.

Fry the ceps in the remaining oil and then nestle them into the rice towards the end of cooking for the last 5 minutes with another splash of stock. Serve straightaway with crusty bread.

Trinxat means to chop or cut in Catalan and is traditionally made with cabbage, potatoes and pork, which reminds me of the comforting British dish bubble-and-squeak. This is on the menu at my restaurant, Pizarro, on Bermondsey Street in London. We make it in the traditional way with jamón ibérico or crispy bacon, but using mushrooms instead makes this a great vegetarian dish.

When it's ready, the *only* way to eat this dish is to mix everything together so that the egg yolks become like a sauce.

Trinxat with duck egg & mushroom stew

Serves 4

500 g (1 lb 2 oz) floury potatoes, cut into bite-size chunks
¼ white cabbage, finely sliced
olive oil for frying
2 banana shallots (eschalions), finely sliced
3 garlic cloves, finely sliced
250 g (9 oz) mixed wild mushrooms
few sprigs of thyme
50–75 ml (1¾–2½ fl oz) fresh vegetable stock
4 duck eggs
sea salt and freshly ground black pepper

Put the potatoes and cabbage in a large pan of boiling water and cook together for 20–25 minutes. Drain the vegetables well and tip into a bowl.

Heat a layer of oil in a pan and fry the shallots for 5 minutes until softened. Then add half of the garlic and cook for a minute more. Add this to the potatoes and cabbage, season well and mix it all up. Once cool enough to handle, shape into eight patties. Chill to firm up for at least 30 minutes.

Heat a little more oil in the pan and add the rest of the garlic, mushrooms and thyme. Cook over a high heat for a few minutes until the mushrooms are tender and golden. Add the stock and seasoning and simmer for 5 minutes.

Heat a layer of oil in a non-stick frying pan and fry the trinxat cakes, in batches if necessary, until golden on both sides and hot in the middle.

Fry the duck eggs in a little oil so that the yolk is still runny. To serve, divide the cakes between four warmed plates, top with an egg and spoon the mushrooms over the top.

chilliman
PENIS PEPPER
100% ORGANIC SEEDS
CAMPEROL
6.90

This recipe is very similar to *pisto*, and I just love it. Pisto is a slow-cooked vegetable stew.

I always serve aubergines (eggplants) this way when I have people round as it's a great dish to share and also to make ahead. My mum is known for cooking her vegetables well, so she will definitely approve of this recipe – it's just her style.

I've used cumin and not pimentón de la Vera, as I would normally do for a pisto, because I think it gives it a nice little twist.

Aubergine stuffed with samfaina

Serves 3–6

3 aubergines (eggplants)
olive oil
2 onions, finely sliced
3 garlic cloves, crushed
2 teaspoons ground cumin
2 red (bell) peppers, sliced
8 large fresh tomatoes, peeled and chopped
30 g (1 oz) unsalted butter
50 g (2 oz) fresh white breadcrumbs
40 g (1½ oz) blanched hazelnuts, roughly chopped
handful of parsley
finely grated zest of 1 lemon
sea salt and freshly ground black pepper

Preheat the oven to 180°C (350°F/Gas 4). Rub the aubergines with oil and roast for 50 minutes to 1 hour until really tender.

Meanwhile, to make the samfaina, heat a good amount of oil in a pan and gently fry the onions for 15 minutes until really lovely and tender. Add the garlic and cumin and fry for a minute.

Stir in the peppers, tomatoes and plenty of seasoning and simmer for 15–20 minutes. Once the aubergines are tender, split in half lengthways, scoop out the flesh (reserving the skins) and roughly chop. Add to the pan and cook for a further 15 minutes.

Heat the grill (broiler) to medium high.

Melt the butter in a separate pan and add the breadcrumbs and hazelnuts, cooking until golden. Season and mix with the parsley and lemon zest.

Fill the aubergine skins with the samfaina mixture, scatter with the crumbs and grill for 2–3 minutes until golden. Serve hot.

I always thought that preserved lemons were from North Africa, and were perhaps introduced to Catalonia by the Moors, but have since discovered that it was very common to make them here long before they arrived.

Feel free to preserve more than two lemons as they keep for a long time and are great for salads or even for some fish stews. You can add them at the end and they will raise the stew to the next level – if you like lemons, of course!

Salad of mató with preserved lemons

Serves 4

2 lemons
3 tablespoons extra virgin olive oil
3 tablespoons caster (superfine) sugar
2 tablespoons flaky sea salt
1 teaspoon black peppercorns
1 whole red chilli
2–3 sprigs of lemon verbena or lemon thyme
handful of baby salad leaves
150 g (5½ oz) fresh raw peas
1 bunch of asparagus, shaved into thin ribbons with a potato peeler
30 g (1 oz) shaved hard Catalan or manchego cheese

for the mató

1 litre (34 fl oz) unpasteurised whole (full-fat) milk
juice of 1 lemon

To make the *mató*, heat the milk in a saucepan until it comes to the boil. Gradually add the lemon juice, a little at a time, until the milk starts to curdle and separate. Use a slotted spoon to scoop the curds into a fine sieve lined with muslin (cheesecloth) set over a bowl. If the water in the pan is still cloudy and not fully separated, you can bring to the boil again and add a little more lemon juice to get all the curds.

Leave the mató to drain overnight so that only the curds are left in the muslin.

Pare the lemons and put the zest in a sterilised Kilner jar. Remove the pith from the lemons, then cut out the wedges and add to the jar. Pour in the extra virgin olive oil and add the sugar, salt, peppercorns, chilli and lemon verbena or lemon thyme. Shake gently to dissolve the sugar, then leave for at least a couple of hours or for up to a week.

To assemble the salad, toss the leaves with the peas and asparagus. Scatter over the mató, hard cheese shavings and some of the preserved lemon segments. Drizzle with the preserving oil and serve.

Robellones (saffron milk cap or red pine mushrooms) grow in abundance throughout Catalonia. I'm also lucky that they were plentiful in my home town of Talaván when I was growing up, so they've always been an ingredient I love to cook with. Just cooked on the plancha and finished with some very finely chopped garlic and parsley with plenty of olive oil and freshly ground black pepper. Heaven!

As for a tortilla, I don't think you can beat this one. If you want to be a bit more adventurous, crumble in some goat's cheese.

Wild mushroom tortilla

Serves 2

olive oil for frying, plus 2 tablespoons for the tortilla
good knob of butter
1 banana shallot (eschalion), finely sliced
2 garlic cloves, finely sliced
3 sprigs of thyme, leaves stripped
350 g (12 oz) wild mushrooms (robellones if you can find them)
handful of chopped parsley
3 large (extra large) free-range eggs
sea salt and freshly ground black pepper

Heat a glug of olive oil and the butter in a pan and fry the shallot for 10 minutes until lovely and soft. Add the garlic, thyme and mushrooms and cook over a high heat for 5 minutes until tender and golden. Remove from the heat and add the parsley.

In a bowl, beat the eggs, then add the mushrooms and plenty of seasoning.

Heat the oil for the tortilla in a 15 cm (6 in) non-stick frying pan. When the oil is hot, add the egg mixture.

Swirl the pan over a high heat until the mixture starts to set around the edges, then reduce the heat and cook for 4–5 minutes until the tortilla just starts to set, the bottom and sides are golden but the middle is still quite loose.

Cover the pan with a flat lid or board and turn the tortilla carefully onto it – don't worry that it is still quite runny; it will all come back together when you continue to cook it. Slide the tortilla back into the pan and, over a low heat, use a spatula to tuck the edges under to give it its characteristic curved look. Cook for a couple of minutes, then turn onto a board and serve. It should still be lovely and juicy in the middle when you cut into it.

For me, calçots are like British asparagus – I can't wait for the season! During the season, you will find great parties called *calçotadas* all over Catalonia. My friend Eduardo says that the calçotadas are like a wedding party, with lots of food and drink.

The traditional method is to put calçots on top of an open fire until the first layers are really burned – they will then cook in their juices, or you can also cook them on a barbecue, under the grill (broiler) or in a heavy-based pan. If you're using a grill, cook them with the flame. Ñora peppers are red, round, sweet-fleshed peppers, normally dried. You'll need to soak them for this recipe.

Calçots

Serves 4–6

12 calçots
olive oil

for the romesco sauce
4 ñora peppers, soaked in boiling water for 1 hour
50 g (1¾ oz) blanched almonds
50 g (1¾ oz) hazelnuts
1 large fresh tomato, peeled
2 garlic cloves
1 slice sourdough
1 tablespoon sherry vinegar
2 piquillo peppers, drained
75–100 ml (2½–3½ fl oz) extra virgin olive oil

Blitz all the ingredients for the romesco sauce together in a food processor until you have a chunky sauce.

Clean the calçots and rub all over with olive oil. Light a charcoal barbecue and add some kindling to get it nice and hot and full of flames, or heat a heavy-based pan or griddle pan over as high a heat as you can.

Sear the calçots all over until browned and tender. Serve with the romesco sauce.

Normally artichokes can be a bit of a pain to prepare, as you need to clean, boil and core them. Here, just cook the artichoke whole and enjoy. I call this 'fun food' and they're great for sharing. I think artichokes and anchovies are a match made in heaven because of the wonderful hit of saltiness and sweetness.

Not exactly Catalonian ... but I don't think you can beat a cold glass of fino with this dish.

Roast artichokes with dipping sauces

Serves 4

4 large globe artichokes, trimmed
juice of 1 lemon
4 tablespoons extra virgin olive oil

for the dips

1 quantity romesco sauce (page 146)

---

100 ml (3½ fl oz) unsalted butter
good grating of nutmeg
sea salt to taste

---

3 tablespoons sherry vinegar
sea salt and freshly ground black pepper
pinch of sugar
75–100 ml (2½–3½ fl oz) extra virgin olive oil

---

6 anchovies
juice of 1 lemon
1 teaspoon Dijon mustard
100–125 ml (3½–4 fl oz) extra virgin olive oil

Preheat the oven to 200°c (400°F/Gas 6). With your fingers, separate the leaves of the artichokes as much as you can. Drizzle with the lemon juice and extra virgin olive oil so they trickle in between the artichoke leaves.

Wrap the artichokes individually in kitchen foil, put in an ovenproof dish and roast for 1 hour to 1 hour 15 minutes.

Meanwhile, prepare the dips. Make the romesco sauce. Melt the butter with a good grating of nutmeg and sea salt and keep warm. Whisk the sherry vinegar with salt, pepper and a pinch of sugar, then gradually whisk in the olive oil. Mash the anchovies with the lemon juice and mustard, season, drizzle in the oil, then whisk to form a thick dip.

Once the artichokes are cooked, unwrap and serve one per person with the dips to dunk into.

This is the salad I prepared for myself and friends when I cook the ox cheeks recipe on page 63. It is a perfect combination and helps cool things down when there's chilli in a sauce, for example.

This is a very popular salad on the menu at Pizarro, where we serve it with some cranberry sauce and goat's cheese. Bliss!

Chicory & pomegranate salad

Serves 4

2 red and 2 green chicory (endive), quartered
olive oil to brush
seeds from 1 pomegranate
1 tablespoon Moscatel vinegar
75 g (2½ oz) dried apricots, chopped
extra virgin olive oil, to drizzle
flaky sea salt

Heat a griddle pan or heavy-based frying pan over a high heat. Brush the chicory with oil and sear until browned.

Mix the pomegranate seeds and their juice with the vinegar, then set aside.

Arrange the chicory on a plate and scatter with the apricots. Drain the pomegranate seeds from the vinegar and scatter over the top. Drizzle with extra virgin olive oil and season to taste with sea salt. Serve immediately.

This dish is well known all over Catalonia, Spain and in tapas bars everywhere.

Whenever I go to a new bar, I always try the *patatas bravas* along with the tortilla, croquetas and jamón ibérico – they're the measure of a good place.

You will find this dish presented and finished in many different ways, but the traditional way is my favourite. Fry the potatoes three times and add the sauce on top. Perfect!

Patatas bravas

Serves 4

olive oil for deep-frying
900 g (2 lb) floury potatoes, peeled and cut into bite-size chunks
flaky sea salt

for the salsa brava
3 tablespoons olive oil
1 onion, finely chopped
2 garlic cloves, crushed
1 red chilli, blackened with a blowtorch or under a very hot grill (broiler) and chopped
400 g (14 oz) tin chopped tomatoes
1 teaspoon smoked pimentón
1 tablespoon sherry vinegar
pinch of sugar
sea salt and freshly ground black pepper

for the alioli
1 free-range egg yolk
½ teaspoon white wine vinegar
75 ml (2½ fl oz) vegetable oil
75 ml (2½ fl oz) olive oil
1 garlic clove, crushed
lemon juice to taste

First make the salsa brava. Heat the oil in a pan and gently fry the onion for 15 minutes until really soft. Add the garlic and cook for a minute more, then add the chilli and tomatoes. Stir in the pimentón, vinegar and sugar, season well and simmer for 20–30 minutes until you have a thick, chunky sauce. Set aside.

To make the alioli, whisk the egg yolk with the vinegar and some seasoning. Gradually whisk in the vegetable, then olive oil in a thin, steady stream, whisking all the time until you have a thick, glossy mayonnaise. Whisk in the garlic and lemon juice to taste. If the alioli is too thick, whisk in 25–30 ml (1 fl oz) of water. Set aside.

Heat a deep pan of olive oil to 100°C (210°F). Fry the potatoes for 10 minutes – they should not be coloured at all at this point. Remove from the pan with a slotted spoon and drain on kitchen paper. Leave to cool completely.

Heat the oil to 160°C (320°F). Fry the potatoes for 4–5 minutes until they are tender and just starting to turn golden. Drain on kitchen paper and leave to cool.

When ready to serve, reheat the salsa brava. Heat the oil to 200°C (400°F) and fry the potatoes for 2–3 minutes until really golden and very crispy. Drain and season to taste with salt. Spoon over the salsa brava and serve with the alioli.

When I start cooking these, I can't stop eating them – they are so delicious. This is a different way to eat artichokes and they taste great with a cold beer.

Membrillo (quince paste) alioli, or *allioli de codony* in Catalan, is typical of the region of Pallars, and makes a good accompaniment to grilled fish and meat, as well as vegetables.

Fried artichokes with membrillo alioli

Serves 4

6 baby globe artichokes
sea salt
squeeze of lemon juice
120 g (4 oz/1 cup) plain (all-purpose) flour
50 g (1¾ oz/scant ½ cup) cornflour (cornstarch)
1 teaspoon baking powder
150–200 ml (5–7 fl oz) sparkling water
olive oil for deep-frying

for the alioli
40 g (1½ oz) membrillo
1 garlic clove
1 free-range egg yolk
2 teaspoons white wine vinegar
pinch of sea salt
150 ml (5 fl oz) olive oil

Clean the artichokes. Slice the stem off a few centimetres before the base and remove and discard a few of the outer leaves. Slice the artichokes very finely with a mandoline and put in a bowl of water with a pinch of salt and a squeeze of lemon juice.

To make the alioli, mash the membrillo and garlic together in a pestle and mortar. Add the egg yolk and vinegar and a pinch of salt. Spoon into a bowl and gradually whisk in the olive oil to form a glossy alioli.

Whisk the flours and baking powder with enough of the sparkling water to make a thick but not clumpy batter. Drain the artichokes and pat them dry with kitchen paper.

Heat the oil in a large pan to 180°C (350°F). Dip the artichoke slices in the batter, then drop into the oil and fry for a minute or two until golden brown. Drain on kitchen paper and season with sea salt. Serve with the alioli.

For me, one of the best things about writing a book is the research, because in doing this, I always find out new and fascinating things. In Girona I discovered one of the most silky goat's cheeses I have ever tasted in my life, called Nuri. This cheese is really creamy and has a delicate, mellow flavour.

It will be difficult to find Nuri outside Girona or even outside the region of L'Empordà, but any good goat's cheese can be used for this dish.

Cured red cabbage with fried goat's cheese & caramelised apples

Serves 4

300 g (10½ oz) soft goat's cheese
2 tablespoons chopped tarragon
3 tablespoons plain (all-purpose) flour
1 free-range egg, beaten
50 g (1¾ oz) panko breadcrumbs
2 apples
40 g (1½ oz) unsalted butter
2 tablespoons caster (superfine) sugar
olive oil for deep-frying
extra virgin olive oil
sea salt and freshly ground black pepper

for the red cabbage

1 medium red cabbage, finely shredded
4 tablespoons flaky sea salt
600 ml (20 fl oz) Moscatel vinegar
130 g (4½ oz) caster (superfine) sugar
1 cinnamon stick

First, cure the red cabbage. Toss the cabbage in the sea salt, then wrap in a clean dish towel and leave in a colander over the sink overnight. Wash, pat dry with kitchen paper and pack into a sterilised jar. Pour in the vinegar and add the sugar and cinnamon. Leave to cure for a minimum of seven days.

Mash the goat's cheese in a bowl with the tarragon and seasoning. Roll into small balls. Put the flour, egg and breadcrumbs in separate bowls. Dip each cheese ball into the flour, followed by the egg and then breadcrumbs. Put on a tray lined with baking parchment and freeze for 20 minutes.

Peel and core the apples and slice into wedges. Melt the butter in a pan and add the apples and sugar and cook, turning, until sticky and caramelised. Transfer the apples to a plate and keep the pan to one side.

Heat the olive oil in a small, deep pan to 180°C (350°F). Fry the cheese balls until golden brown, then remove with a slotted spoon and drain on kitchen paper. Season with sea salt.

Drizzle some extra virgin olive oil into the still warm apple pan.

Drain some of the red cabbage and arrange on small plates. Top with the apples and fried goat's cheese balls, then spoon over the sweet extra virgin olive oil.

To me, seeing these mushrooms means spring has arrived. The last time I cooked with these I was in the Basque country with my dear friends Juan Mar Arzak and Jose from Ganbara.

We were cooking in a *sociedad gastronómica*, which is a gastronomic gentlemen's club, and there was a debate about whether the mushrooms taste better when small or big in size. We all agreed that the bigger ones have a much better aroma and flavour.

Chickpeas with Saint George's mushrooms

Serves 4

320 g (11½ oz) dried Spanish chickpeas (garbanzos), soaked overnight in cold water
1 tablespoon olive oil for frying
20 g (¾ oz) unsalted butter
300 g (10½ oz) St George's mushrooms, sliced
100 ml (3½ fl oz) fino sherry
4 free-range eggs
handful of watercress

for the stock
1 carrot, cut into pieces
1 onion, quartered
1 celery stalk
handful of black peppercorns
2 bay leaves
few sprigs of thyme

To make the stock, put the vegetables, peppercorns and herbs in a large pan and add 1.7 litres (3 pints) of cold water. Bring to the boil and simmer for 20 minutes. Strain and return the stock to the pan.

Drain the chickpeas and add to the stock. Cook for 1 hour until the chickpeas are completely tender and the stock is absorbed, but they are still a little bit juicy.

Meanwhile, heat the oil and butter in a pan and fry the mushrooms for 5 minutes over a high heat. Add the sherry and bubble for a minute.

Poach the eggs in simmering water until set but the yolks are still runny. Stir the watercress into the chickpeas, then divide between four warmed bowls. Top each with a poached egg and some mushrooms and serve.

I think this dish, *habas a la brutesca*, is a winner. It's baby broad (fava) beans cooked on hot coals until blackened (see the picture on the previous page). Then the beans are simply popped from their pods to make the salad. Here I'm using jamón, but you could use your favourite cheese for a vegetarian version. Why not make both?

Habas a la brutesca

Serves 4

1 kg (2 lb 4 oz) broad (fava) beans in their pods
125 g (4½ oz) jamón, torn
2 tablespoons shredded mint
good squeeze of lemon juice
extra virgin olive oil, to drizzle
sea salt and freshly ground black pepper

Heat a barbecue with lots of charcoal. You will need a long length of thin wire, or you could use metal skewers. Thread the bean pods onto the wire, curling the wire around into a spiral. Put the spiral of beans into the hot coals and cook until they are blackened.

Cool the beans a little, then pop them out of their pods into a bowl. Mix with the jamón, mint, some lemon juice and plenty of extra virgin olive oil. Season and serve.

I've had this recipe on the menu at my restaurants for many years on and off. Normally, I sauté spinach very quickly. However, in this recipe I suggest cooking for a longer time until the spinach is really well cooked. This is the way my friend Pilar cooked the dish for me at El Rebost de la Cartoixa, with plenty of garlic!

Remembering other good times, I have tried a recipe from my friend José Andres where he added some apple – this was a really great combination and I'd recommend that depending on what you like.

Catalan spinach

Serves 4

2 tablespoons olive oil
4 garlic cloves, peeled
100 g (3½ oz) raisins
3 tablespoons pine nuts
2 kg (4 lb 7 oz) baby spinach
sea salt and freshly ground black pepper

Heat the oil in a pan. Add the garlic and cook for 1 minute. Add the raisins and pine nuts and cook for a minute or two until the pine nuts start to turn golden. Add the spinach and sauté until wilted and well cooked. Season to taste and serve.

This is a very simple recipe in Catalan cuisine, known as *Pa amb tomàquet* – a slice of bread with tomatoes, some salt and olive oil. Sometimes you can toast the bread and rub in some garlic. The story is that this is a good way to use up old bread, as the tomatoes and olive oil bring back moisture – makes sense to me!

In my restaurants, we toast a type of light bread, then rub in some garlic. We then rub the tomatoes over the garlic bread, add a good glug of olive oil and some salt. We buy our tomatoes from Catalonia where they are called 'hanging tomatoes', because they are kept hanging for the whole year.

Pan con tomate

Serves 2

4 slices white bread cut from a loaf
1 garlic clove, peeled
4 ripe tomatoes, halved
extra virgin olive oil, to drizzle
flaky sea salt

Lightly toast the bread, then rub each slice with the garlic clove. Put two tomato halves, cut side down, on each slice and press down with your fingers, squeezing the insides over the bread (discard the outside). To serve, drizzle with oil and sprinkle with sea salt.

Cartoixa d'Escaladei is a monastery in the mountains of Montsant, Priorat. It is a really idyllic place that you must visit – the ruins will transport you back to a time when monks were living and praying there. I can imagine them picking wild asparagus, the same way I did on my last visit.

This is a very simple combination but really succulent – serve it alone or as a garnish for fish or meat.

Wild asparagus with peas & morels

Serves 4

200 g (7 oz) fresh peas
2 large bunches (approx. 500g/ 1 lb 2 oz) of wild or regular asparagus, trimmed
2 tablespoons olive oil for frying
1 banana shallot (eschalion), finely sliced
1 garlic clove, finely sliced
200 g (7 oz) morels
good squeeze of lemon juice
extra virgin olive oil, to drizzle
sea salt and freshly ground black pepper

Blanch the peas and asparagus in boiling water for a minute until just tender. Drain and refresh under cold water.

Heat the oil in a pan and fry the shallot for 10 minutes until tender. Add the garlic and morels and fry for 3–4 minutes until the mushrooms are tender. Season to taste and then add the asparagus and peas and toss together to warm through.

Tip into a serving bowl and drizzle with lemon juice and extra virgin olive oil before serving.

Desserts

I know that not everyone has a sweet tooth but for many people having dessert is a really important part of a meal. There are even those who like to enjoy a dessert on its own from time to time. I have friends who say they think a meal is not really complete without a dessert and they'll even check the dessert menu before choosing their starter or main dish. I think it's really fun to treat ourselves to something sweet, and have one (or two) of our favourites!

I've noticed that different people like different levels of sweetness too – so choosing the right dessert is important. Some desserts might be a simple combination of fruit using mainly natural sugars, while others have just a little sugar to sweeten them. Then there are those for people who like a really big, full-on sugar blowout! The type of sugar you use will also create very different flavours and textures, but whatever your preference, I hope you'll enjoy the desserts I'm putting on the menu here in this gorgeous chapter especially for you from Catalonia.

As you reach the edge of the province of Tarragona, just before you hit the region of Valencia, you'll find the Delta del Ebro. I think this area produces the best clementines in the whole of the Iberian Peninsula – they have the perfect balance of sweetness and acidity. They are called *Clementinas de las Tierras del Ebro*, and they're protected by the government.

I really love to mix cava with this clementine sorbet. These are two great Catalonian gems together – just divine!

Clementine sorbet

Serves 4

150 g (5½ oz/⅔ cup) caster (superfine) sugar
100 g (3½ oz) honey
14 clementines
1 lemon
1 blood orange, skin removed and cut into slices, to serve (optional)

Melt the sugar and honey in a pan with 250 ml (8 fl oz) of water. Bring to the boil and then boil for 5 minutes. Set aside to cool.

Squeeze the juice from all the fruit and sieve it into a jug – you need about 350 ml (12 fl oz) of juice. When the syrup is cold, stir in the juice and taste for sweetness, adding a little more honey if you want to sweeten.

Churn in an ice-cream maker until softly set,then spoon into a tub and freeze completely. If you don't have an ice-cream maker, pour into a wide container and freeze for 1 hour, then mash with a fork and freeze for another hour and repeat until you have a soft sorbet before freezing completely. Serve a scoop of sorbet with some slices of blood orange, if using.

These *carquinyols* are just so good that it's hard to stop eating them once you start. My mum always tells me not to eat them when they're still warm … but I just can't resist. Sorry, Mum!

Carquinyols are a double-baked biscuit, very similar to the Italian *cantuccini* biscuits that I also love with a coffee.

Marinating the almonds in the alcohol gives a great flavour to the biscuit and here I use anise liqueur, but use any that you like since the result will be the same.

Carquinyols

Makes 20

120 g (4 oz) whole blanched almonds
50 ml (1¾ fl oz) anise or any other liqueur
1 large (extra large) free-range egg
100 g (3½ oz/scant ½ cup) caster (superfine) sugar
175 g (6 oz/scant 1½ cups) plain (all-purpose) flour
finely grated zest of 1 orange
1 teaspoon baking powder (baking soda)
pinch of ground cinnamon
pinch of sea salt

Preheat the oven to 180°C (350°F/Gas 4).

Soak the almonds in the anise for 10 minutes (or you can soak in water). Beat the egg and sugar together until pale and fluffy, then fold in the flour, orange zest, baking powder, cinnamon and salt.

Drain the almonds and fold in. Divide the dough in half and roll into two sausage shapes. Put on a baking tray lined with baking parchment and cook for 30 minutes until very lightly golden.

Remove and, while still warm, cut into 5-mm (¼-in) thick slices. Place these flat (cut side up) on the baking tray and return to the oven for a further 5 minutes until golden brown and crunchy. Leave to cool on a wire rack.

ANTIQUARI
BAR
JIM BEAM
BOURBON

I have experimented with different flavours over the years, trying crema Catalana with coffee, cardamom, vanilla and more. But in the end, I think the traditional one is the best.

In Pizarro Restaurant, I love to burn the sugar with a traditional hot plancha, which gives off a gorgeous aroma. Heaven!

Crema Catalana

Serves 8

1 litre (34 fl oz) whole (full-fat) milk
pared zest of 1 lemon and 1 orange
½ small cinnamon stick
6 large (extra large) free-range egg yolks
60 g (2 oz/¼ cup) caster (superfine) sugar, plus extra to caramelise
40 g (1½ oz/⅓ cup) cornflour (cornstarch)

Put the milk, zests and cinnamon in a pan and bring to the boil, then set aside to infuse for at least 1 hour. When cold and infused, strain through a fine sieve (strainer).

Beat the eggs and sugar together until thick, pale and fluffy, then beat in the infused milk and cornflour.

Pour into a clean pan and cook over a low heat for 10 minutes, stirring constantly, until you have a thick custard. Sieve into a jug and pour into eight dishes or large ramekins. Chill in the fridge for at least 3 hours, or overnight, until completely set.

When ready to serve, sprinkle a layer of sugar over the top and caramelise quickly with a blowtorch, or under a very hot grill (broiler). Chill again for at least an hour before serving.

I always cook quince in red wine or cava, with a few spices added too. I thought it was about time I gave *vermut* (vermouth) a try, given it's such a traditional drink in Catalonia. It was a bit of a revelation! I've used some of the botanicals from the vermouth here as well, to really elevate the vermouth itself, and I think they just bring the whole dish together really nicely.

Quince cooked in vermouth

Serves 8

4 quinces, peeled, cored and halved
juice and pared zest of 1 lemon
650 ml (23 fl oz) vermouth
200 g (7 oz/scant 1 cup) caster (superfine) sugar
12 cardamom pods
few sprigs of dried or fresh marjoram

Put the quinces in a bowl of cold water with a little lemon juice to stop them discolouring.

Put the vermouth, 600 ml (20 fl oz) of water, the sugar, cardamoms, marjoram and lemon zest in a pan and simmer until the sugar dissolves. Drain the quinces and add to the pan, cover with a piece of baking parchment and simmer gently for 30–45 minutes until the quinces are tender when pierced with the tip of a knife.

Remove from the heat and set aside to cool in the liquid. Pour one-third of the cooking liquid into another pan and boil hard until it has reduced to a lovely syrup. Serve the quince halves with the syrup. This is amazing with the *crema Catalana* on page 184, or just on its own.

Candied fruits were some of my dad's most favourite things ever. I still remember his face when I took him to Fortnum & Mason for the first time – he was in heaven. I suspect I have the same look when I go to La Boquería market.

Sometimes when I'm in the middle of the process, I think it might not be worth making your own candied fruit, but once you've tried some of your own efforts, hopefully you'll agree they're completely worth it.

I use this method to make all sorts of candied fruit.

Whole candied oranges

Makes 6

6 medium oranges
1.4 kg (3 lb 1 oz/6¼ cups) caster (superfine) sugar
6 tablespoons golden (light corn) syrup or glucose

Pierce the oranges all over with a fine needle, to allow the syrup to get right into the middle.

Boil the oranges in a pan of water for 1 hour to soften the skins and remove some bitterness. Drain and set aside.

Put the sugar, syrup or glucose and 2.8 litres (5 pints) of water in a pan and heat gently until the sugar dissolves. Add the oranges and partially cover with a lid. Bring to the boil, then gently simmer for 1 hour. Remove from the heat, cover completely and leave for 24 hours.

The next day, bring back to the boil, partially cover and gently simmer for 30 minutes. Set aside and leave for 24 hours. You need to repeat this process every day for the next six days. If the syrup reduces too much, add a little water to the pan.

Once finished, the oranges will keep in the fridge in an airtight container for up to six months.

Use the whole fruit to make the *Bizcocho* recipe on page 193. The syrup can be used for the ice cream on page 194.

Once you've made lots of candied fruit (page 191), you'll want to find more things to do with it, and I think this cake is the perfect home for the candied orange you've got to hand.

This recipe is very similar to one my sister, Isabel, cooks all the time, but I have adapted it to include oranges, which takes it to another dimension altogether.

Bizcocho with candied orange

Serves 8

175 g (6 oz/scant 1½ cups) plain (all-purpose) flour
2 teaspoons baking powder (baking soda)
125 g (4½ oz) caster (superfine) sugar
pinch of salt
100 g (3½ oz) ground almonds
1 candied orange (page 191)
200 ml (7 fl oz) extra virgin olive oil
3 large (extra large) free-range eggs
100 ml (3½ fl oz) orange juice
icing (confectioner's) sugar, to dust

Preheat the oven to 170°C (340°F/Gas 4). Grease and line a 900 g (2 lb) loaf pan.

Sift the flour into a bowl and stir in the baking powder, sugar, salt and almonds. Make a well in the centre.

Whiz the whole orange in a food processor with the olive oil to make a paste, then pour into the dry ingredients. Add the eggs and orange juice and beat together to make a smooth batter.

Pour into the loaf pan and bake for 50–60 minutes until risen and golden and a skewer inserted into the centre comes out clean. Leave to cool in the pan for 10 minutes, then remove to a wire rack to cool completely. Serve dusted with icing sugar.

This is a classic ice cream in my house, and the first time I made it, it was very sweet for me (I'm sweet enough!).

I gave some thought as to how I could keep the sweetness, but give it some contrast too, and the bitters just seemed to make perfect sense.

Candied orange syrup & bitters ice cream

Serves 4–6
Makes 700–750 ml (24–25 fl oz)

300 ml (10 fl oz) whole (full-fat) milk
300 ml (10 fl oz) double (heavy) cream
100 g (3½ oz/scant ½ cup) caster (superfine) sugar
4 large (extra large) free-range egg yolks
8 generous tablespoons orange syrup (from the candied oranges, page 191)
2 good shakes of bitters

Put the milk and cream in a pan and bring to the boil.

Whisk the sugar and egg yolks until light and fluffy, pour over the hot cream mixture and stir well. Strain back into a clean pan and cook until you have a thick custard that coats the back of a spoon. Leave to cool, then chill in the fridge overnight.

The next day, churn the ice cream in an ice-cream maker. When almost set, gradually pour in the orange syrup and add the bitters. Mix with a spatula, then churn for a minute or two more until set. Spoon into a container and freeze completely.

If you don't have an ice-cream maker, pour into a tub and freeze for 1 hour, then whisk with an electric hand whisk. Repeat this twice more and on the third whisk, gradually whisk in the orange syrup and add the bitters. Freeze for another hour and whisk for a final time, then freeze until solid.

I'm going to let you in on a secret: when I'm on holiday I really love to have these hazelnut and plum cakes for breakfast, served with a *carajillo*. Carajillo is a Spanish way of taking coffee with either whisky, brandy, anisette or rum. It's a good way to start the day on holiday, so why not?

Hazelnuts are cultivated widely throughout Catalonia. For me, they're the best bedfellow for plums, and so these little cakes of joy were born!

Hazelnut & plum cakes

Makes 6

120 g (4 oz) unsalted butter, softened
150 g (5½ oz/⅔ cup) caster (superfine) sugar
3 free-range eggs
180 g (6 oz/1½ cups) self-raising flour, sifted
75 g (2½ oz) ground hazelnuts
60 ml (2 fl oz) extra virgin olive oil
3–4 ripe plums, stoned and chopped
icing (confectioner's) sugar, to dust

Preheat the oven to 180°C (350°F/Gas 4). Grease and line six mini loaf pans.

Beat the butter and sugar together until light and fluffy. Gradually add the eggs, one at a time, beating constantly. Fold in the flour, nuts and olive oil until you have a smooth batter, then fold in the plums.

Divide between the mini loaf pans then place on a baking tray and bake for 20–25 minutes or until a skewer inserted into the centre of a cake comes out clean. Cool in the pans for 5 minutes, then turn out onto a wire rack. Dust with icing sugar and serve warm with cream.

One of the good things about the end of spring and the beginning of summer is the arrival of all the fruit – strawberries are one of my favourite fruits. British strawberries are among the best in the world, but some types of Catalonian strawberries are fragrant and juicy too, in a different way.

This is one of the simplest recipes ever, and adding the vinegar makes it really refreshing and delicious for summertime.

Strawberries with vermouth vinegar

Serves 4

400 g (14 oz) strawberries, hulled and halved
120 ml (4 fl oz) vermouth vinegar
70 g (2½ oz/⅓ cup) caster (superfine) sugar
3–4 sprigs of lemon verbena or lemon thyme

Put the strawberries in a dish and cover with the vinegar, sugar and lemon verbena or lemon thyme. Mix and set aside to macerate for a couple of hours before serving.

The picture of these *magdalenas* just takes me right back to being a child and coming home from school. My mum would always have one of these or some chocolate on toast waiting for me. I used to sit on the step at my grandmother's house and eat very slowly. My grandmother used to get very cross with me for that – you have to eat the magdalenas warm!

Magdalenas

Makes 12

4 free-range eggs
170 g (6 oz/¾ cup) caster (superfine) sugar, plus extra to sprinkle
120 ml (4 fl oz) extra virgin olive oil
200 g (7 oz/1⅔ cup) plain (all-purpose) flour
1 teaspoon baking powder
finely grated zest of 1 lemon

Preheat the oven to 180°C (350°F/Gas 4). Line a 12-hole muffin pan with cupcake cases.

Beat the eggs and sugar together until really light and fluffy. Gradually whisk in the olive oil, then fold in the flour, baking powder and lemon zest.

Divide the batter between the cases, sprinkle with some extra sugar and bake for 18–20 minutes until risen and golden. Cool slightly on a wire rack. Serve warm.

This is a traditional cake that a godfather gives to the godchild on Easter Sunday after church. However, it can be made and served at any time, from the most basic events to the most elaborate occasions. Having said that, I still think this recipe is most complete and yummy when it's just a simple chocolate recipe.

One thing I love to do in Barcelona is to walk from one patisserie to another, just to see the creations of incredibly gifted pastry chefs. It's as good as walking around different art galleries – at least you can put this art in your mouth and taste the genius!

Monas de Pascua

Serves 4

500 g (1 lb 2 oz/4 cups) plain (all-purpose) flour, plus extra to dust
10 g (½ oz) sea salt
15 g (½ oz) fresh yeast or 7 g (¼ oz) sachet fast-action dried yeast
100 ml (3½ fl oz) warm water
3 (large) free-range eggs, beaten, plus 1 for glazing
80 ml (2¾ fl oz) olive oil
175 g (6 oz/¾ cup) caster (superfine) sugar
finely grated zest of 1 orange and 1 lemon
4 hard-boiled free-range eggs
melted dark chocolate and sugar strands to decorate

Sift the flour and salt into a bowl. Mix the yeast with a little of the warm water and leave to stand for 10 minutes until frothy.

Make a well in the centre of the flour and add the yeast mix and the rest of the water, together with the beaten eggs, oil, sugar and zests. Using your hands, bring the mixture together into a really soft dough. Knead with the dough hook in a stand mixer or by hand, lifting and stretching the dough out of the bowl until it is smooth and elastic and no longer really sticky – this will take about 5–10 minutes in a machine or 10 minutes by hand.

Place in a lightly greased bowl, cover and leave in a warm place until doubled in size – this could be anything from 2–4 hours.

Tip the dough onto a lightly floured surface, divide into four pieces and roll into balls. With your fingers, make a hole in the centre of each ball, so they look like large doughnuts. Put a hard-boiled egg in the centre of the dough. Place on two lined baking trays, cover with a clean dish towel and leave to rise for 1 hour.

Preheat the oven to 180°C (350°F/Gas 4). Brush the monas with the beaten egg for glazing and bake for 20–25 minutes until golden and risen.

Remove from the oven and leave to cool on a wire rack. Drizzle with the melted chocolate, scatter with sugar strands and serve.

Turrón is very famous and very popular. There are so many different varieties too – hard, soft, with egg yolk, with coconut. But you can only really find it at Christmas, which is annoying as I love chocolate turróns so much. Just a little piece after a meal with my espresso makes me happy.

Look, I had to do something about that situation, so I've created this recipe – no more waiting until Christmas.

Chocolate turrón

Makes 20 pieces

150 g (5½ oz) whole blanched almonds
50 g (1¾ oz) peeled pistachios
2 sheets wafer paper
200 g (7 oz) honey
200 g (7 oz/scant 1 cup) caster (superfine) sugar
1 large (extra large) free-range egg white
1 tablespoon cocoa (unsweetened chocolate) powder

Preheat the oven to 170°C (325°F/Gas 3). Line a baking tray with baking parchment and roast the nuts until they are lightly golden brown. Check on them regularly as they catch really easily. Set aside to cool.

Line an 18 cm (7 in) square tin with a layer of wafer paper.

Put the honey and sugar in a pan over a low heat. Melt the sugar, then bring to a rapid boil and cook until the mixture reaches 120°C (250°F) on a sugar thermometer.

Beat the egg white in a stand mixer until it holds soft peaks, then, while whisking, gradually pour in the hot sugar and honey mixture.

Once the egg white is all incorporated, scoop the mixture back into the pan and put over a medium-low heat, stirring constantly. The aim is to reduce the moisture content of the nougat and, when the mixture reaches about 150–155°C (300–310°F) on a sugar thermometer, start testing it. Drop a little bit into a bowl of cold water – it should harden into a ball immediately.

When this happens, add the nuts and cocoa powder to the turrón. Mix well, then pour into the lined tin and smooth with a palette knife. Top with a second layer of wafer paper and leave to set completely before slicing.

Brazo de Gitano, or 'Gipsy's Arm', is derived from the Swiss roll. The history of this dessert is said to stretch back to medieval times when it was brought to Spain by an Italian monk from Egypt. It's one of my favourite desserts.

Persimmon fruit are more popularly called *kaki* in Catalonia and although they are very popular at every single market, I do love to see them at La Boquería – there's something about the way they're presented and organised.

Feel free to substitute the compote for any jam or sweet filling.

Brazo de gitano

Serves 6

4 large (extra large) free-range eggs, separated
100 g (3½ oz/generous ¾ cup) caster (superfine) sugar, plus extra to sprinkle
1 teaspoon vanilla bean paste or extract
100 g (3½ oz/generous ¾ cup) plain (all-purpose) flour
1 teaspoon baking powder (baking soda)
pinch of fine sea salt
300 ml (10 fl oz) double (heavy) cream
icing (confectioner's) sugar, to dust

for the compote

5 persimmons, flesh mashed
1 small apple, peeled, cored and chopped
½ teaspoon ground ginger
1 tablespoon caster (superfine) sugar
1 tablespoon lemon juice

Preheat the oven to 180°C (350°F/Gas 4). Grease and line a 33 × 22 cm (13 × 8½ in) Swiss roll tin (pan).

In a stand mixer, beat the egg yolks, sugar and vanilla paste or extract until really pale and fluffy and the mixture holds a ribbon shape for a few seconds when you stop whisking.

Sift the flour, baking powder and salt together and fold into the egg yolks. Beat the egg whites until they form stiff peaks. Carefully fold them into the batter, then spoon into the Swiss roll pan and spread out with a spatula.

Bake for 10–12 minutes until just cooked. Put a clean dish towel on the worktop and cover with a piece of baking parchment. Sprinkle the paper with sugar. Turn the still-warm sponge out onto the sugared paper and peel off the baking parchment from the bottom.

While still warm, roll up the sponge using the dish towel to help you, and making sure the paper rolls on the inside of the sponge. Set aside to cool.

To make the compote, put the fruit, ginger and sugar in a pan and cook together until the fruit has broken down. Whiz using a hand-held blender until smooth. Add the lemon juice and cool completely.

When ready to serve, unroll the sponge and remove the paper. Lightly whip the cream until just holding its shape and spread all over the sponge. Spoon the compote over the top of the cream and roll the sponge up again. Dust with icing sugar and serve.

This is the typical dessert prepared for enjoying on Saint's Day in Catalonia. There are just so many variations on this dessert, and you can use sweet or normal potatoes. I prefer sweet potatoes.

Some people think that the use of the potatoes is just to make the recipe cheaper, but I don't agree with that. For me, the potatoes give this dessert a much lighter texture.

Panellets

Makes 25

400 g (14 oz) potatoes or sweet potatoes (about 3)
300 g (10½ oz) ground almonds
100 g (3½ oz/scant ½ cup) caster (superfine) sugar
finely grated zest of 1 lemon
2 free-range eggs, separated
300 g (10½ oz) pine nuts

Preheat the oven to 200°C (400°F/Gas 6). Prick the potatoes all over and roast for 25–30 minutes until tender. Remove from the oven and, when cool enough to handle, scoop the flesh into a bowl – you should have about 300 g (10½ oz).

Add the ground almonds, sugar and lemon zest and mix well.

Shape into small balls, about 120 g (4 oz) each. Beat the egg whites until foaming and beat the egg yolks in a separate bowl. Roll the balls in the egg whites, then coat all over with pine nuts and place on a baking tray lined with baking parchment. Brush with the beaten egg yolks and bake for 10–12 minutes until golden brown.

I've made saffron ice cream many times, and each time I do, I find I make a little change to the recipe. Here's my best one so far.

I had some pine nuts left over from my recipe for *Panellets* (page 215) and I thought I'd try adding them to the saffron ice cream. Well, they take the ice cream to another level, giving it a really earthy flavour that goes extremely well with those panellets.

Saffron & pine nut ice cream

Serves 4–6
Makes 700–750 ml (24–25 fl oz)

pinch of saffron threads
300 ml (10 fl oz) whole (full-fat) milk
300 ml (10 fl oz) double (thick) cream
100 g (3½ oz) pine nuts
125 g (4½ oz/generous ½ cup) caster (superfine) sugar
4 large (extra large) free-range egg yolks

Put the saffron in a pan with the milk and cream. Bring to the boil, then remove from the heat and leave to infuse for 1 hour.

Toast the pine nuts in a dry pan until just golden. Allow to cool, then whiz in a food processor with the sugar. Add the eggs and whiz again to form a smooth paste.

Strain the saffron cream over the egg mixture and mix well, then pour back into the pan and cook until you have a thick custard that coats the back of a spoon. Leave to cool, then chill in the fridge overnight.

The next day, churn the ice cream in an ice-cream maker until set. Then scoop into a container and freeze until solid. If you don't have an ice-cream maker, then pour into a tub and freeze for 1 hour before whisking with an electric hand whisk. Repeat this three more times, then freeze until solid.

Don't think *coca* here means the same as cocoa. Coca can be sweet or savoury, and this sweet version is delicious. If you've made the candied fruits (page 191), you're probably still looking for more ways to use them up. Of course, you can use any summer fruits as well. Enjoy!

Sweet coca

Serves 6

12 g (1/2 oz) fresh yeast or 7 g (1/4 oz) sachet fast-action dried yeast
330 ml (11 1/2 fl oz) lukewarm water
pinch of sugar
500 g (1 lb 2 oz/4 cups) plain (all-purpose) flour, plus extra to dust
10 g (1/2 oz) fine sea salt
finely grated zest of 1 lemon
1 tablespoon extra virgin olive oil, plus extra to brush
1 free-range egg yolk
2 tablespoons caster (superfine) sugar, plus extra to sprinkle
fine polenta, to dust

to serve
500 g (1 lb 2 oz) candied fruit such as oranges, pineapple, cherries, lemon (page 191), sliced
70 g (2 1/2 oz) toasted pine nuts

Cream the yeast in a bowl with a little of the water and a pinch of sugar. When smooth, add three-quarters of the remaining water and leave to stand, covered, for 30 minutes until the mixture starts to bubble.

Sift the flour and salt into the bowl of a stand mixer. Add the yeast and the rest of the ingredients apart from the polenta and knead with the dough hook for 5 minutes on a low speed, adding more of the water if it looks a little dry. Leave to stand for 10 minutes, then knead again for 5 minutes until smooth and elastic. Cover and stand for 1 hour or until doubled in size.

Divide the dough into six equal portions, then roll out on a lightly floured surface into 30 cm (12 in) tongue-like shapes. Sprinkle two baking trays with a little polenta, place the dough pieces on top, cover with a clean dish towel and stand in a warm place for 15 minutes.

Preheat the oven to as high as it will go. Brush the dough bases lightly with olive oil and sprinkle with sugar. Bake for 10–12 minutes, or until the bases are golden and crisp. Serve warm with the candied fruit and pine nuts sprinkled on top.

Tortosa is a really stunning city in the South of Catalonia, a place you must try to visit. These delicious pastries are stuffed with pumpkin jam – in other parts of Spain they're called *cabello de ángel* which, in English, means 'angel's hair'! The name is likely to have arisen as a result of cooking the pumpkin (squash) in the sugar, which is the way you make it, and it looks like beautiful golden hair.

It can be difficult to find the Siam pumpkins but don't worry because you can easily buy them as well as tins of *cabello de ángel* online.

Pastisset de anis or tortosa

Makes 10

500 g (1 lb 2 oz/4 cups) plain (all-purpose) flour
1 teaspoon baking powder
75 ml (2½ fl oz) olive oil
100 ml (3½ fl oz) anise or any aniseed-flavoured liqueur
100 ml (3½ fl oz) sweet wine
75 g (2½ oz) unsalted butter, softened
10 heaped tablespoons cabello de ángel (pumpkin jam)
1 large (extra large) egg, lightly beaten
caster (superfine) sugar, to sprinkle

Sift the flour and baking powder into a bowl and make a well in the centre. Mix the oil, anise and sweet wine together and pour into the well with the softened butter. Bring together and knead for 10 minutes until you get a fine and elastic dough that isn't sticky. Leave to stand for 20 minutes.

Preheat the oven to 200°c (400°f/Gas 6) and line a baking tray with baking parchment.

Divide the dough into ten x 80 g (3 oz) balls. Roll the balls out (without extra flour) into 12 cm (4¾ in) circles.

Spoon a generous tablespoon of cabello de ángel into the middle of each circle of dough. Brush the edges with beaten egg, fold over to make a half moon and press to close, sealing with a fork.

Put the pastissets on the baking tray and brush with the beaten egg. Bake for 18–20 minutes until golden. Allow to cool a little, then coat with sugar and serve warm.

Well, this recipe name literally translates to 'drunks'! These cakes have been made by my friend Enric's family since 1929. Enric is the third generation at Faixat Pujadas Patisserie in Barcelona, and we first met when working together in London. I respect his pastry skills so much and admire him as a friend. When he took on the family business it was traditional and he chose to develop it in a new direction, taking a more innovative and modern approach.

These cakes are really addictive – you can't have just one!

Borrachos de almendra

Makes 16

for the cakes

3 eggs, plus 3 egg yolks
75 g (2½ oz) marzipan, grated
125 g (4½ oz/scant ⅓ cup) caster (superfine) sugar
250 g (9 oz/scant 1¼ cup) plain (all-purpose) flour, plus extra to dust

for the meringue

6 egg whites
75 g (2½ oz/scant ⅓ cup) caster (superfine) sugar

for the sugar syrup

200 g (7 oz/scant 1 cup) caster (superfine) sugar
200 ml (7 fl oz) anise or any aniseed-flavoured liqueur

for the egg yolk cream

635 ml (21 fl oz) whole (full-fat) milk
2 vanilla pods (beans), split lengthways
10 large (extra large) free-range egg yolks
150 g (5½ oz/⅔ cup) caster (superfine) sugar
25 g (1 oz/¼ cup) plain (all-purpose) flour
25 g (1 oz/¼ cup) cornflour (cornstarch)

Heat the oven to 180°C (350°F/Gas 4). Grease and flour a 30 × 20 cm (9 × 13 in) rectangular cake tin (pan).

In a stand food mixer, beat the whole eggs, yolks, marzipan and sugar until smooth and fluffy. Fold in the flour.

To make the meringue, in a clean bowl, whisk the egg whites to stiff peaks, then add the sugar a little at a time, whisking until you have a glossy mixture. Fold this carefully into the cake mix.

Spread the mixture into the tin. Bake for 30–35 minutes until golden and firm to the touch. Allow to cool.

To make the sugar syrup, melt the sugar and anise together and bubble until you have a thin syrup. Allow to cool.

To make the egg yolk cream, pour the milk into a small saucepan along with the vanilla pods and heat until beginning to steam but not boiling. Remove the vanilla pods and set aside.

In a medium-sized bowl, whisk together the egg yolks and sugar along with the flours. Whisk in a third of the vanilla milk, then transfer to the saucepan of remaining vanilla milk. Heat the mixture over a medium heat and whisk continuously until thickened. Allow to bubble for a minute, then set aside to cool.

Slice the entire cake horizontally in half. Brush one half of the cake with the sugar syrup, and using a blowtorch, evenly caramelise until golden brown. Spread over a quarter of the topping and sandwich together with the other piece of cake. Slice into 9 x 2 cm (3½ × ¾ in) rectangles. Transfer the cream to a piping bag fitted with a medium-sized round nozzle and pipe the remaining topping onto each cake to decorate. Serve.

To be honest, I have no idea where the name Sara comes from in this recipe title. Even my friend Enric doesn't really know (although there are different versions), and this cake has been sold in his patisserie in Barcelona for almost 100 years!

I just fell in love with these little cakes when I tried them. You know when you try a new food and it brings back good memories? This is what happened to me with Sara de almendra. They remind me of the bread and butter with plenty of sugar that my mum, Isabel, used to give me after school when I was a child – which tasted better than it sounds! Of course, these cakes are far more yummy.

Sara de almendra

Makes 16

for the cake

6 eggs
180 g (6 oz/generous ¾ cup) caster (superfine) sugar
150 g (5½ oz/scant 1¼ cups) plain (all-purpose) flour
2 tablespoons cornflour (cornstarch)
2 tablespoons almond flour
zest of ½ lemon
½ teaspoon baking powder
200 g (7 oz) toasted flaked (slivered) almonds, to decorate

for the buttercream

185 g (6½ oz/generous ¾ cup) caster (superfine) sugar
125 g (4½ oz) egg yolks
250 g (9 oz) unsalted butter, softened
1 teaspoon vanilla bean paste

for the sugar syrup

100 g (3½ oz/scant ½ cup) caster (superfine) sugar
70 ml (2¼ fl oz) anise or any aniseed-flavoured liqueur

Preheat the oven to 180°C (350°F/Gas 4). Grease and flour a 30 × 20 cm (9 × 12 in) rectangular cake tin (pan).

To make the cake, beat the eggs and sugar together until light and fluffy and leaving a ribbon trail in the mixture. In a separate bowl, sift the flours together, then fold them into the egg mixture a little at a time. Fold in the lemon zest and baking powder.

Carefully pour the mixture into the cake tin and bake for 20–25 minutes until risen and golden. Cool for 10 minutes in the tin, then turn out onto a wire rack to cool completely.

To make the buttercream, put the sugar and 75 ml (2½ fl oz) of water in a pan and melt over a low heat. Bring to the boil and cook until you reach short thread stage: 114°C (237°F) on a sugar thermometer. Put the egg yolks in a stand mixer and beat as you pour in the hot sugar syrup. Keep beating until the mixture has cooled completely. Gradually beat in the softened butter and vanilla until you have a thick, glossy butter icing.

To make the sugar syrup, melt the sugar and anise together and bubble until you have a thin syrup. Allow to cool.

Trim off any uneven edges of the cake, then cut into 9 × 2 cm (3½ × ¾ in) rectangular portions. Briefly dip the tops of each cake into the sugar syrup, then place on a wire rack. Spread the butter icing over the top and sides of the cake, coat in toasted flaked almonds and serve.

Orejitas means 'little ears' because of the shape of these little cakes, and they are, in fact, very similar to *coquillos* in Extremadura.

It's a real shame that something as gorgeous as these sugar-dusted cakes seem to be increasingly difficult to find nowadays. Okay, I know this might be because they're normally fried, and possibly a bit unhealthy, but please give me a break! Think of this as a real treat or something to have with a cortado. If you're in the UK, you might have just found the perfect treat to have with your cup of tea!

I'd love you to try this really tasty recipe. I'd eat them all!!

Orejitas with honey & anise

Makes 7

250 g (9 oz/scant 1¼ cups) plain (all-purpose) flour, plus extra to dust
20 g (¾ oz) baking powder
finely grated zest of 1 lemon
1 teaspoon ground cinnamon
25 g (1 oz) unsalted butter, softened
20 g (¾ oz) caster (superfine) sugar, plus extra to dust
good pinch of salt
1 egg
110 ml (3¾ fl oz) whole (full-fat) milk
1.5 litres (3 pints) vegetable oil, to fry

for the syrup
200 g (7 oz) honey
100 ml (3½ fl oz) anise or any aniseed-flavoured liqueur

Put the flour, baking powder, lemon zest and cinnamon in a bowl with the butter, sugar and salt. In a separate bowl, mix the egg and milk together. Add to the flour mixture and bring together into dough. Knead for 10 minutes until you have a smooth, elastic dough.

Lightly flour a baking sheet. Divide the dough into seven × 60 g (2 oz) portions and roll into balls, place on the baking sheet and leave in a warm place, covered with lightly oiled cling film (plastic wrap), for 1 hour 15 minutes or until doubled in size.

Meanwhile, make the syrup. Heat the honey and anise together until you have a light syrup. Keep warm.

Heat the oil in a deep pan to 170°C (340°F/Gas 3) or until a cube of bread browns in 30 seconds. Roll out the dough balls to as thin a disc as you can. Deep-fry them one at a time for 1–2 minutes, turning, until golden brown and puffed. Drain on kitchen paper, then brush with the warm syrup and place on a cooling rack over a baking sheet to drain off any excess. Dust in sugar and serve.

Catalan menus

Cooking a Catalonian feast for friends and family can also be fun if you know how to plan. Many dishes can be prepared in advance, which takes the stress out of cooking on the day and means you can actually enjoy yourself! I have listed four menus here to get you started, which are suitable for either four or six guests.

Menu 1

Serves 6

Black pudding & apple croquetas (page 19)
Trotter sliders (page 30)
Clams 'a la plancha' with olive oil (page 125)
Razor clams with jamón & cava vinaigrette (page 86)
Catalan spinach (page 167)
Strawberries with vermouth vinegar (page 199)
Saffron & pine nut ice cream (page 216)

Two or more days before

- Cook the trotters for the sliders and allow them to cool in their liquid.
- Make the alioli and romesco sauces, spoon into sterilised jars or containers and chill.
- Make the ice cream and freeze in a container.

The day before

- Make the mix for the croquetas and shape into balls, place on a lined baking sheet and chill.
- Shred the trotters to make the mix for the sliders. Shape into burgers and chill.
- Prepare the razor clams. Steam them, then remove the meat. Put in a bowl and cover and chill.

On the day

- Heat the oil and fry the croquetas.
- Fry the sliders and assemble in the buns.
- Cook the spinach.
- Cook the clams.
- Fry the jamón and make cava vinaigrette; add the prepared razor clams to the jamón and heat through.
- Marinate the strawberries.

Menu 2

Serves 4

Chicken cannelloni (page 60)
Roast monkfish tail with lemon thyme salsa (page 99)
Clementine sorbet (page 178)

Two or more days ahead

- Make the sorbet and freeze in a container.

The day before

- Make the meat filling and sauce for the cannelloni, put into airtight containers and chill.
- If you are pressed for time, you can make the lemon thyme salsa, store it in an airtight container and chill, though try to make it on the day if you can.

On the day

- Fill the cannelloni with the meat mixture and place in an ovenproof dish. Warm through the sauce, pour over and bake.
- Bake the monkfish tail.

Menu 3

Serves 6

Whole roasted cauliflower with anchovy sauce (page 112)
Fricandó of beef with pied bleu mushrooms & black olives (page 49)
Crema Catalana (page 184)

The day before

- Make the fricandó of beef. Allow to cool in the casserole, then chill.
- Make the anchovy sauce for the cauliflower, spoon into an airtight container and chill.
- Make the crema Catalana and chill.

On the day

- Reheat the beef in the casserole for 30–40 minutes.
- Caramelise the crema Catalana and re-chill for at least an hour.
- Roast the cauliflower, slice and fry the leaves and warm the sauce.

Menu 4

Serves 4

Pan con tomate (page 170)
Gambas carpaccio (page 104)
Bacallà a la llauna, spinach & piquillo peppers (page 77)
Hazelnut & plum cakes (page 196)

The day before

- Make the cakes, cool and store in an airtight container.
- Marinate the tomatoes for the gambas and leave in a cool place overnight.

On the day

- Slice the prawns (shrimp) and assemble the carpaccio.
- Make the pan con tomate.
- Cook the bacallà a la llauna.

QUALITE EXTRA

Places to eat in Barcelona:

Bar La Plata
Chef Santino
Carrer Mercè, 28,
08002 Barcelona
www.barlaplata.com

Tickets Bar
Chef Albert Adrià
Avinguda del Paral·lel, 164,
08015 Barcelona
www.ticketsbar.es/en

Quimet & Quimet
Joaquim Pérez
Carrer del Poeta Cabanyes, 25,
08004 Barcelona

La Cova Fumada
Josep María y Magí Sole
Carrer Baluard, 56,
08003 Barcelona

Faixat Pujadas Pastisser
Enric Christensen
Carrer de Muntaner, 159-161,
08036 Barcelona
www.faixatpujadas.com

El Suquét de l'Almirall
Chef Quim Marqués
Passeig de Joan de Borbó, 65,
08003 Barcelona
www.suquetdelalmirall.com

El Quim de la Boqueria
Chef Quim Márquez
Mercado de La Boqueria,
La Rambla, 91,
08001 Barcelona
www.elquimdelaboqueria.com

Outside Barcelona:

Restaurant Casa de Fusta
Chef Elisabet Bo i Escala
Partida L'Encanyissada
S/N 43870 Amposta, Tarragona
www.restaurantcasadefusta.com

El Rebost de la Cartoixa Restaurant
Chef Pilar del Olmo
Rambla Cartoixa, 15,
43379 Scala Dei, Tarragona
www.elrebostdelacartoixa.com

Restaurant Miramar
Chef Paco Pérez
(2 Michelin Stars)
Passeig Marítim, 7,
17490 Llançà, Girona
www.restaurantmiramar.com/en

La Tancada
Parcela 83,
Poligono 78,
Contrada Sant Carles de la
Rapita Salines
S/N 43870 Amposta, Tarragona

El Celler de Can Roca
Chef Joan Roca
(3 Michelin Stars)
Carrer de Can Sunyer, 48,
17007 Girona
www.cellercanroca.com

VETERANO
CARLOS III
CUTTY SARK
BLENDED SCOTCH WHISKY
LICOR
TRIPLE
Magno
RARE
J&B
BLENDED SCOTCH WHISKY
SOBERANO
Ron Pujol
ANIS DEL MONO
VICENTE BOSCH
BADALONA
43
TORRONS I DOLÇOS
Planelles - Donat

Acknowledgements

This book would not have been possible without the direct and indirect help of many people.

To the whole team working on the book: Kate Pollard, my publisher, for making sure it happened. Lizzie Kamenetzky for your help with developing and tasting the recipes, and your enormous patience! Laura Edwards and Kendal Noctor for the visual gift you have, amazing eye and sensitivity for light and shade, and colour – you capture the best photographs! Also, Polly Webb-Wilson for her brilliant props. All the team at Hardie Grant, especially Kajal Mistry, Emma Marijewycz, Caroline Proud and Margaux Durigon. Designer Clare Skeats and illustrator Stephen Smith.

To Zoraida Martinez and Demelza Marquez for making my life easier.

Special thanks to the Delegation of the Government of Catalonia to the United Kingdom and Ireland, and to the Spanish Tourist Office.

My dear friends Eduardo De Felipe and Lara Viejo for all your help and time researching with us. To the most welcoming of friends, and great hosts, Gloria and Carlos from Mas Rabiol – you must stay and eat sometime! To my long time friend Enric from Pastiseria Faixat Pujadas, my favourite patisserie in Catalonia.

To Josep Cuní for sharing your stories and regional knowledge of places, culture and history.

Huge thank you to Maruja Molina Calà and Florian Pi Romaní, who are like my family in Catalonia. Thanks for your time, great food and your knowledge. José Miguel Fábregas and Lola Hervàs, for showing us around the beautiful Delta del Ebro.

To the many restaurants we visited, thank you for spending time cooking for and with us, especially El Rebost de Cartoixa, and thank you in particular to Pilar Del Olmo, Merce Piñol and Fernado Piñol. Camping at La Tancada, especially Pepe Montañes and Josep and Xavier Montañes. My thanks to Casa de Fusta, particularly Luis Garcia and Elisabeth Bo. To all the stunning markets, and a special mention to La Boqueria in Barcelona, one of my all-time favourites – particular thanks to Oscar Ubide.

And to Quico Cost, for keeping Cala Estreta impeccable.

To all the teams in all four restaurants – you're amazing people, and I appreciate the work you do.

About the author

José Pizarro has lived in the UK for 18 years and in that time has worked at some of London's most prestigious Spanish restaurants, including Eyre Brothers, Brindisa and Gaudi.

He owns four restaurants in London – José, Pizarro, José Pizarro and Little José, which opened its doors in 2017.

In 2014 José was voted one of '100 españoles' – a hugely prestigious award, which showcases the top 100 Spaniards around the world, based on how they have brought their talents to the masses and demonstrated their Spanish pride through their work.

Index

D

E

Q

R

S

A note on oven temperatures: If you are using a fan-assisted oven, please reduce the oven temperatures in the recipes by 20°C (36°F/1 or 2 Gas marks).

Quadrille, Penguin Random House UK, One Embassy Gardens, 8 Viaduct Gardens, London SW11 7BW

Quadrille Publishing Limited is part of the Penguin Random House group of companies whose addresses can be found at global.penguinrandomhouse.com

Published by Quadrille in 2025
First published in 2017 by Hardie Grant
www.penguin.co.uk

A CIP catalogue record for this book is available from the British Library

ISBN 9781784887735
10 9 8 7 6 5 4 3 2 1

First edition

Publisher: Kate Pollard
Senior Editor: Kajal Mistry
Editorial Assistant: Hannah Roberts
Publishing Assistant: Eila Purvis
Design and Art Direction: Clare Skeats
Photography: © Laura Edwards
Photography Assistant: Kendal Noctor
Home Economist: Lizzie Kamenetkzy
Prop Stylist: Polly Webb-Wilson
Copy Editor: Lorraine Jerram
Home Economist: Lizzie Kamenetkzy
Prop Stylist: Polly Webb-Wilson
Proofreader: Delphine Phin
Indexer: Cathy Heath

This edition

Publishing Director:Kajal Mistry
Senior Commisisoning Editor: Kate Burkett
Cover, chapter openers and illustrations:
Double Slice
Copy Editor and Proofreader: Caroline West
Production Manager: Sabeena Atchia

Colour reproduction by p2d

Printed in China by C&C Offset Printing Co., Ltd

The authorised representative in the EEA is Penguin Random House Ireland, Morrison Chambers, 32 Nassau Street, Dublin D02 YH68.

Penguin Random House is committed to a sustainable future for our business, our readers and our planet. This book is made from Forest Stewardship Council® certified paper.